IMPROVING BOARD RISK OVERSIGHT THROUGH BEST PRACTICES

IMPROVING BOARD RISK OVERSIGHT THROUGH BEST PRACTICES

By

Paul L. Walker,
William G. Shenkir,
and
Thomas L. Barton

The Institute of Internal Auditors
Research Foundation

Disclosure

Copyright © 2011 by The Institute of Internal Auditors Research Foundation (IIARF), 247 Maitland Avenue, Altamonte Springs, Florida 32701-4201. All rights reserved. No part of this publication may be reproduced, stored in a retrieval system, or transmitted in any form by any means — electronic, mechanical, photocopying, recording, or otherwise — without prior written permission of the publisher.

The IIARF publishes this document for informational and educational purposes. This document is intended to provide information, but is not a substitute for legal or accounting advice. The IIARF does not provide such advice and makes no warranty as to any legal or accounting results through its publication of this document. When legal or accounting issues arise, professional assistance should be sought and retained.

The Institute of Internal Auditors' (IIA's) International Professional Practices Framework (IPPF) comprises the full range of existing and developing practice guidance for the profession. The IPPF provides guidance to internal auditors globally and paves the way to world-class internal auditing.

The mission of The IIARF is to expand knowledge and understanding of internal auditing by providing relevant research and educational products to advance the profession globally.

The IIA and The IIARF work in partnership with researchers from around the globe who conduct valuable studies on critical issues affecting today's business world. Much of the content presented in their final reports is a result of IIARF-funded research and prepared as a service to The Foundation and the internal audit profession. Expressed opinions, interpretations, or points of view represent a consensus of the researchers and do not necessarily reflect or represent the official position or policies of The IIA or The IIARF.

ISBN 978-0-89413-714-3
9/11
First printing

Contents

List of Tables and Figures vi
Acknowledgments vii
About the Authors ix
Executive Summary xi
Introduction THE ROAD TO RISK OVERSIGHT BY THE BOARD 1
Scope of Interviews 5
Best Practices 7
Chapter 1   BOARD'S DISCUSSION OF RISK AND ERM 9
Chapter 2   KNOW THE BUSINESS AND ITS INDUSTRY 11
Chapter 3   BOARD MEMBERS' SKILLS AND EXPERIENCES 15
Chapter 4   DOCUMENTING BOARD RISK OVERSIGHT 17
Chapter 5   STRATEGY, STRATEGIC RISK, AND ERM 21
Chapter 6   INDICATING RISK VELOCITY ON A RISK MAP 25
Chapter 7   ERM TRAINING FOR THE BOARD AND MANAGEMENT 27
Chapter 8   SCANNING AND RECALIBRATION OF RISKS 29
Chapter 9   RISK REPORTING 33
Chapter 10   ERM PROCESS 39
Chapter 11   RISK FRAMEWORK 45
Chapter 12   BOARD AND C-SUITE RELATIONSHIP 49
Chapter 13   THE BOARD AS A RISK 53
Chapter 14   INTERNAL AUDITING 57
Conclusion 63
Appendix A: Summary of Best Practices 65
Appendix B: Board Assessment of Risk Oversight and ERM: A Tool 67
Appendix C: Summary of CAE/Internal Audit's Role in Board Risk Oversight Best Practices 69
Appendix D: Interview Protocol 73
Notes 75
The IIA Research Foundation Sponsor Recognition 79
The IIA Research Foundation Board of Trustees 80
The IIA Research Foundation Committee of Research and Education Advisors 81

List of Tables and Figures

Figure 1: Board Committee Risk Assignments 18

Figure 2: Risk Management Alignment Guide Example 19

Figure 3: The COSO ERM Cube 46

Figure 4: Roles the Internal Auditor Can Do, Can Do with Safeguards, and Cannot Do with Respect to Risk Management 58

Acknowledgments

The authors would like to thank the many internal auditors, board members, and risk managers who gave so freely of their time, knowledge, and insight. Arranging and completing the lengthy interviews required a significant commitment on their parts, and we are most grateful for this. We wish we could identify and thank each individual by name, but we are bound by our confidentiality agreements, and so we thank them collectively.

We would also like to thank the members of The Institute of Internal Auditors' (IIA's) Committee of Research and Education Advisors review team for their diligence and wise counsel:

Thomas Beirne, AES Corporation

John C. Harris, Aspen Holdings

Frank O'Brien, Olin Corporation

Richard Anderson (Trustee Champion), DePaul University

The many pages of interview transcription were produced quickly and accurately by the crack team of Lauren Walker, Sarah Till, and Shirley Barton. We are most grateful to them.

Finally, we sincerely thank The IIA Research Foundation (IIARF) — especially former Operations Manager Nicki Creatore — for their commitment to improving risk management and making the world a safer place.

About the Authors

Paul L. Walker, PhD, CPA, is an associate professor of accounting at the University of Virginia's McIntire School of Commerce and director of the PricewaterhouseCoopers Center for Innovation in Professional Services. Dr. Walker co-developed one of the first courses on enterprise risk management (ERM) in the world. He has taught ERM at the University of Virginia to numerous executive groups and boards. Dr. Walker also served as a visiting fellow at the London School of Economics Centre for the Analysis of Risk.

He was one of the original consultants to the Committee of Sponsoring Organizations of the Treadway Commission (COSO) on its ERM process and framework and served as an advisor to both small and large organizations on ERM, including the Federal Reserve Bank, several Fortune 500 companies, a leading university, and international companies. Additionally, he has been invited to train international audiences on ERM, including companies with operations in South Korea, Japan, and Belgium.

Dr. Walker has coauthored numerous publications on ERM, including *Making Enterprise Risk Management Pay Off* and *Enterprise Risk Management: Pulling it All Together*. He has also coauthored several articles on ERM, including "Managing Risk: An Enterprise-Wide Approach," "A Road Map to ERM," and "ERM and the Strategy-Risk Focused Organization."

William G. Shenkir, PhD, CPA, is the William Stamps Farish Professor Emeritus at the University of Virginia's McIntire School of Commerce, where he served on the faculty for almost 40 years and as the dean from 1977 to 1992. He continues to be involved in research and consulting on ERM. In this area, he has coauthored research studies funded by the Financial Executives Research Foundation, Institute of Management Accountants, The Institute of Internal Auditors Research Foundation, and the Bureau of National Affairs. He also served as a consultant to COSO on its ERM project, co-developed a graduate ERM course, and has spoken on ERM before numerous professional groups in the United States and abroad.

He has published more than 60 articles in academic and practitioner journals, made more than 100 presentations before professional and academic organizations, and edited or coauthored eight books. From 1973 to 1976, he served as a technical advisor and project director at the Financial Accounting Standards Board (FASB). Dr. Shenkir served as president of the Association to Advance Collegiate Schools of Business International (AACSB) and as a vice president of the American Accounting Association (AAA).

Dr. Shenkir has served on numerous professional committees of the AAA, American Institute of Certified Public Accountants (AICPA), Financial Executive Institute (FEI), and the Virginia Society of CPAs. He is currently serving as chair of the AICPA International Qualification Examination Committee (IQEX) and on the CPA Examination Content Committee. He has also taught executive development programs for personnel from industry, government, and accounting firms.

He currently serves on the Board of Directors and audit and compensation committees for ComSonics, Inc. He has previously served as a member of the Board of Directors of Dominion Bankshares Corporation, the Deloitte & Touche Academic Advisory Board, and First Union National Bank — Mid-Atlantic Region.

In 1995, he received the Virginia Outstanding Educator Award from the Carman Blough Chapter of the IMA, and in 1997, he was recognized as one of the 10 University of Virginia Distinguished Professors in the students' yearbook, *Corks and Curls*.

Thomas L. Barton, PhD, CPA, is Kathryn and Richard Kip Professor of Accounting at the University of North Florida. He holds a PhD in accounting from the University of Florida and is a certified public accountant (CPA). Dr. Barton has more than 50 professional publications, including research articles in *Barron's*, *Decision Sciences*, *Abacus*, *Advances in Accounting*, *Financial Executive*, *CPA Journal*, and *Strategic Finance*, and five books and one audio book, which was nominated for *Audio Book of the Year*. He received the Lybrand Silver Medal for his article, "A System is Born: Management Control at American Transtech."

He is the creator of the Minimum Total Propensity to Disrupt method of allocating gains from cooperative ventures. This method has been the subject of several articles in *Decision Sciences*. He is also a recognized expert in the application of management controls to highly creative activities.

Dr. Barton has taught more than 150 professional development seminars and has extensive consulting experience with a wide cross section of organizations in the public and private sectors. He is the recipient of several teaching awards for his undergraduate and graduate work. He was a winner of the State University System of Florida's prestigious Teacher Incentive Program award in the program's inaugural year.

Executive Summary

The world is a very risky place, as documented constantly in news reports. Boards are under pressure as never before to ensure that the management of their organizations is identifying and managing the major risks. Government regulators, credit rating agencies, and the various stakeholders are, in effect, demanding that major risks be managed better.

Enterprise risk management (ERM) is a relatively new tool available to tame the risky environment facing organizations. It is an integrated approach to risk management, avoiding the old inefficient and oftentimes ineffective silo approach — strategic, operational, financial, and hazard risks each managed separately in their own compartments or "silos." There have been significant strides in ERM design and execution over the last few years while ERM has been widely available as a discrete management tool.

One area of ERM that has remained relatively underdeveloped is in board oversight of risk management. Although the U.S. Securities and Exchange Commission (SEC) has expanded board risk disclosures, it is clear that much work remains to be done. Our purpose with this study is to identify and document best practices that major organizations have developed in improving board risk oversight. We believe that other organizations will benefit from considering these best practices for their own use.

To this end, we interviewed chief audit executives (CAEs), board members, and directors of ERM to find out what their organizations are doing in this area, especially with respect to the contribution of internal auditors. All 23 organizations are U.S.-based and publicly traded. They represent a wide cross section of industries and, in some cases, are leaders in their sectors. Some of the organizations are from the Fortune 100.

In the Best Practices section of the report, we discuss our findings under 14 categories. We list the best practices in Appendix A but strongly encourage readers to read the detailed comments and insights that led to the practice. The best practices include how the board can become a risk if it does not have a variety of skills, the expertise needed to match the business, and the required knowledge of the business. The best practices also include a discussion of the importance of board committee risk assignment and more recent developments in risk management, such as incorporating velocity into risks, conducting deep dives on the risks, and recalibrating the risks. Best practices also include training the board, risk frameworks and risk reporting via dashboards or maps, and the delicate relationship between the CEO and board that is so vital to risk management and risk oversight.

Our discussion in each category is relatively detailed and concludes with a specific best practice (or practices). We include quotations from our interviewees as a way to not only share their insights but also to reveal thought processes and the general tone of their approaches.

The resulting list of best practices is fairly comprehensive. Of course, no one company is using all of the best practices. But a reasonable goal for any organization is to adopt as many best practices as will comfortably fit within its culture and structure.

Risk management is an evolutionary process. Even early ERM adopters have made significant changes to their systems over the years as they learned what works and what doesn't work — and what makes for a better-managed organization. Of course, some have learned the hard way as their "model" ERM systems didn't meet the challenges of the recent financial crisis and other roadblocks.

Some organizations initially tried to manage risks enterprise-wide without a formal process. However, most companies and boards figured out that good risk oversight requires a well-developed ERM system. Without this world-class, more formalized ERM process, it is easier to not identify major risks, to not see the links between the risks, and to miss the strategic side of risk management. As a result, we include Appendix B for boards to use to begin assessing and reviewing their own ERM and risk oversight processes. It is not necessarily a list of "if you do these 25 things, you will have a world-class ERM process." Instead, Appendix B should be used to ignite the conversation about risks in your organization. Board members can take the list of questions and ideas in Appendix B and ask themselves whether they are following that approach — and if not, then why not.

Of course, many boards may come to realize that they need significant help in improving both their ERM systems and their risk oversight processes. As such, we summarize in Appendix C how internal auditors and CAEs might play a role in the best practice or in the assessment process. We found that many CAEs are critical players in the risk process and can add value. We also found that most of them are part of a highly connected networked group that openly shares best techniques for ERM and frequently improves their risk processes by learning best practices and tools from other organizations going through the same challenges. Boards may want to consider tapping into this deep reservoir of knowledge.

It is especially gratifying to us that we found a number of executives and board members who were willing to share their insights to help other organizations bolster their risk management processes and improve board risk oversight.

Introduction

THE ROAD TO RISK OVERSIGHT BY THE BOARD

> Boards must now exercise risk oversight as never before.
> — National Association of Corporate Directors[1]

Because the goal of enterprise risk management (ERM) is to "create, protect, and enhance shareholder value," ERM should be of vital concern to every board overseeing an organization, regardless of the industry or country.[2] However, the road to that conclusion has not always been clear and is littered with confusion from the U.S. Securities and Exchange Commission (SEC), the courts, and even sidetracked United States Senate bills. ERM infancy is somewhat hard to trace, but some early published works include *Risk Management: Changing the Internal Auditor's Paradigm*,[3] *A Conceptual Framework for Integrated Risk Management*,[4] and the field research studies *Making Enterprise Risk Management Pay Off* and *ERM: Pulling it All Together*.[5, 6]

These later two books documented how leading organizations were implementing an ERM process. This early work also led to some key insights with respect to successful ERM, including foundational elements of a successful ERM program. Those early elements included C-level support and chief audit executive (CAE) leadership, a focus on value, changes in internal auditing, ownership versus facilitation, ERM infrastructure, integration of risks, and corporate governance.

Internal auditors played an early role in ERM in part because some mistakenly saw ERM as part of the U.S. Sarbanes-Oxley Act of 2002 but also because internal auditors needed to play a role, given their extensive knowledge of the business, its processes, risks, and controls. The fact that not many organizations had chief risk officers (CROs) in ERM's infancy also led to a greater role for the CAE.

After these early pioneering studies, two events emerged to change ERM. First, in 2000, The Committee of Sponsoring Organizations of the Treadway Commission (COSO) engaged a team of researchers whose task was to determine whether a new framework (beyond *Internal Control – Integrated Framework*) was needed in today's riskier environment.[7] The consultants recommended that COSO develop an enterprise-wide risk framework that would help organizations create value and help future professionals, regulators, and boards manage risk. COSO responded to that advice and produced *Enterprise Risk Management – Integrated Framework* in 2004.

As ERM evolved, so did the stated role of the internal auditor in risk management. In 2001, The IIA published the *Standards for the Professional Practice of Internal Auditing* (*Standards*) (effective in 2002), constructed around a "value-added" definition of internal auditing. This new definition replaced a controls and compliance-oriented definition that dated back to 1947.[8]

The revised definition states:

> Internal auditing is an independent, objective assurance and consulting activity designed to add value and improve an organization's operations. It helps an organization accomplish its objectives by bringing a systematic, disciplined approach to evaluate and improve the effectiveness of *risk management*, control, and governance processes.[9] [Emphasis added]

In concert with the updated definition, the new *Standards* clearly establish a more "pro-active role for internal auditors in risk management and governance processes."[10] The previous *Standards* focused on the internal auditor as a provider of assurance. By contrast, the new *Standards* distinguish between the assurance (A) and nonassurance or consulting (C) services. For example, Section 2010 on Planning contains implementation subsections 2010.A1 ("... plan of engagements should be based on a risk assessment") and 2010.C1 ("The chief audit executive should consider accepting proposed consulting engagements based on the engagement's potential to improve management of risks, add value, and improve the organization's operations.")[11]

As to the evolution of ERM, the second major event occurred around the time of the COSO work. After a series of high-profile business failures, the Sarbanes-Oxley Act was passed in 2002 and a series of SEC changes began to consume U.S. businesses. There was some confusion after Sarbanes-Oxley — some thought it mandated ERM, while others thought it mandated just internal control over financial reporting. Adding to the confusion was the fact that COSO now had two frameworks. The confusion was also caused by certain sections of Sarbanes-Oxley. Section 302 mandated disclosure controls but also suggested some organizations needed "an assessment and evaluation of operational and regulatory risk" — clearly going beyond just internal controls over financial reporting.

Section 404 of Sarbanes-Oxley added to the confusion by suggesting that companies have controls over the risk assessment process and that the board should approve policies over business control and risk management practices (again, note the broader scope of risks suggested here). Businesses sought guidance and others implored the SEC to make it clearer.[12] Eventually the SEC had to take a position and state that it did not intend to mandate ERM or a specific control framework (at least that was not the intent in 2004).[13] Despite the SEC's position and emphasis just on financial reporting and related internal control, the SEC began to mandate risk factor disclosures in Item 1a of the 10-K around 2007.

Still, outside of the SEC's views, others were raising the bar and asking deeper questions about organizations, boards, and risk management. One area raising the bar was the listing requirements for companies on the New York Stock Exchange (NYSE). The NYSE's listing requirements stated that the CEO and senior management were responsible for assessing and managing risk and that the audit committee must discuss the guidelines and policies to govern the process.

The road to ERM adoption was paved a bit more with Standard & Poor's announcement of the incorporation of a review of a company's ERM practice into their ratings process — explicitly meaning that the ERM review would influence the company's credit rating and presumably its cost of raising capital. Senator Charles Schumer (New York) became involved by proposing a shareholder bill of rights and the establishment of risk committees. The bill suggested that boards had failed their "basic duty" to oversee enterprise risk. The bill did not make progress but received a great deal of attention and, once again, altered the conversation about the role of boards in ERM.

Additional pressure on directors came from the Disney and Caremark court rulings that significantly expanded directors' oversight duties. A recent Harvard Law Forum stated: "While we expect that the business judgment rule will survive the financial crisis intact, boards and companies should remain mindful in the current environment of the possibility that courts may apply new standards, or interpret existing standards, to increase board responsibility for risk management."[14]

Another forum addressing this topic suggested: "Boards should ensure that the company implements appropriate reporting and monitoring systems tailored to each type of material risk." The forum added that "the board should periodically review and ask management or outside consultants to assess the system's adequacy" (to avoid potential Caremark liability).[15] As a result, one lawyer and NYSE board member stated, "Bottom line is that directors breach the duty of loyalty by having a known duty to act and by ignoring it. Risk oversight is a board duty."

Adding to this fiduciary pressure was the fact that many *non*-U.S. regulators viewed ERM as mandatory for both management and boards long before the SEC issued its new risk oversight rules. For example, the independent regulatory bodies and the stock exchange requirements in the United Kingdom suggest a greater role over risk and risk management for both the board and management than is suggested in the United States: The board's role is to provide leadership to enable risk to be assessed and managed.[16]

A U.K. board is also required to consider the nature of risks, the categories of risk, the likelihood of risk, and the company's ability to manage the incidence and impact of the risks.[17] Additionally, the European Union has issued guidance that links enterprise risk management to the board, particularly the audit committee.[18] Other countries have taken a similar approach, including South Africa and Australia. In fact, Australia has principles of good corporate governance and one prominently listed principle is "recognizing and managing risk."[19]

Why should U.S. boards look at how other countries are managing risk? First, as stock exchanges merge and global markets converge, some of these risk differences will need to be addressed. If a company wants to operate or become listed in another country, it needs to know the corporate governance requirements in that country. Second, and more importantly, companies are competing in a global market. Investors can move their money with a few computer clicks, implying that companies that better manage their risks may be more attractive than those that take risks and risk oversight casually. In fact, the South African corporate governance guidance states, "The proper governance of companies will become as crucial to the world economy as the proper governing of countries."[20]

Of course, the current economic meltdown and the stories about companies taking huge risks (e.g., AIG, British Petroleum, and Washington Mutual) that potentially led to their downfall or had huge negative impacts on their business may have been the proverbial straws that broke the camel's back and prodded the SEC to step up the risk efforts. For starters, the SEC created a new division to focus on systemic risks. Next, it released Final Rule 33-9089: Proxy Disclosure Enhancements (which was effective 2/28/10). That rule mandated board risk oversight disclosures, disclosure of the risk reporting lines, and reporting and linking of compensation practices to risk taking. Of course, for boards to properly oversee risk, management needs to first implement an ERM process.

More recently, the Dodd-Frank Act of 2010 raises the bar for financial institutions in the ERM area. The Act requires all public, nonbank financial companies supervised by the Federal Reserve and all public, bank-holding companies with more than US $10 billion in assets to have a risk committee. That committee is to oversee the enterprise-wide risk management practices. The committee is also supposed to include the number of independent directors as the Board of Governors of the Federal Reserve System deems appropriate. Finally, the risk committee is required to have at least one risk management expert (similar to the Sarbanes-Oxley requirements for financial experts). The expert should have experience in ERM areas such as risk identification and risk assessment.

All of these factors have brought boards and executives to the point that ERM and risk oversight not only are required but are considered the right way to do business. Only fools operate without knowing their risks. Nonetheless, ERM and risk oversight is new to many companies, and best practice has been slow to be recognized.

Some help was offered by the COSO ERM framework. COSO clearly lays out the purpose and the close relationship between the board and management in an ERM approach: "Achievement of strategic objectives and operations objectives, however, is subject to external events not always within the entity's control; accordingly, for these objectives, enterprise risk management can provide reasonable assurance that management, and the board in its oversight role, are made aware, in a timely manner, of the extent to which the entity is moving toward achievement of the objectives."[21]

As is evident, the board, in its oversight role, can help management implement an ERM process. What is also clear is the purpose of the ERM effort — to help organizations know whether they are on track to meet their objectives, both strategic and operational. All board members want their organizations not only to have the right objectives and strategy but also to meet those objectives. Having a world-class ERM process and risk oversight in place is one way to gain additional assurance on meeting objectives.

Scope of Interviews

In this study, the researchers conducted 18 interviews involving 20 interviewees who were all with public companies in the United States. The interviewees included 10 board members, six chief audit executives (CAEs), one internal auditor who headed the North American audit team of a global organization, and three directors of enterprise risk management (ERM). In two instances, a board member and the CAE of the same organization were interviewed. Because several board member interviewees served on more than one board, 23 different organizations were represented from the following business sectors: energy, engineering, financial services, food services, health care, manufacturing, pharmaceutical, retail, and software.

In arranging the interviews, the researchers sent — in advance — an Interview Protocol to each interviewee (see Appendix D). The interview approach was not literally to focus on each question but rather to have a conversation about board risk oversight processes, with the questions providing some general background for the interviewee. Before each interview, the researchers asked permission to tape the interview and informed the interviewee that no information would be attributed to them or their organization in the final report. Therefore, to maintain confidentiality, no quotes in this report are attributed to any interviewee or their organization.

Best Practices

In this section, we present and discuss the best practices of the study companies in engaging their boards in the enterprise risk management (ERM) effort. Of course, not all companies include all of the practices in their own risk management systems. But the practices we include are readily accepted and time-tested aids to making the ERM systems more effective and to strengthening the oversight of risk by boards.

We organize the discussion in a series of subsections dealing with specific topical areas. Where appropriate, we have included quotes from our interviewees that help advance an understanding of the systems and why they are successful.

Throughout the section, we show best practices in bold print. In Appendix A, we present a separate summary list of the best practices we identified for boards. Appendix C shows a summary of the roles of chief audit executives (CAEs) and internal audit professionals in each of these risk oversight best practices.

Chapter 1

BOARD'S DISCUSSION OF RISK AND ERM

A frequently cited practice among the board members interviewed was that at least annually the senior management makes an "in-depth" or "deep dive" presentation to the entire board on the significant risks facing the organization. The presentation usually includes a heat map and substantial backup information on the significant risks and action plans related to those risks. Such presentations provide an opportunity for the board to accomplish two objectives: 1) to understand how management implemented ERM and the process that management uses to identify, assess, and monitor the risks; and 2) to question management on the significant risks facing the organization. While this annual presentation is important, in evaluating such a presentation, one board member stated:

> I think that this presentation has some use; if nothing else, it demonstrates that management is thinking about the issues that the businesses have. I don't think that the process alone is sufficient to feel comfortable that the board is providing the oversight that it needs to provide. The presentation is certainly one element in the program. I wouldn't describe that as the element that says: "If you do this, don't worry about anything else."

A practice to assure that management is continuously focused on the risks facing the organization is for the board to request that the annual presentations be updated at quarterly board meetings. This practice enables a board to determine what the trend is in management's risk assessment and to perform its risk oversight responsibilities at other board meetings. One director, reviewing the process at his company, stated, "We will focus on changes during the year — additions, subtractions — and so at the rest of the board meetings we're pretty much looking at the heat map — any changes since the last report. They always review our top five risks. And we have a dashboard. And we have a sheet on planned actions."

One of the CAEs noted that they initially reported annually to the audit committee the top 10 risks. However, the CAE does a survey each year asking the audit committee members if they are "presenting the right topics to them." As part of the survey, the committee was asked, "What they'd like to see more of, less of, and every single one of them said you know, we really want to see those top 10 lists quarterly which has really probably become a best practice now."

From the interviews, a best practice is: **Management should present to the board annually a deep dive on the ERM process and on the significant risks facing the organization and should provide updates of the significant risks and the related action plans at the quarterly board meetings.**

For CAEs and audit professionals: **Internal auditors 1) could make the board presentation or be present when management presents the risks; 2) should be ready to answer board questions related to the risks; 3) could provide assurance on the information provided by management; and 4) could provide updates on the status of management's action plans.**

In considering the risk information reported to a board, a critical question is: How can a board be confident it is receiving the right quantity and best quality of risk information? Two ways suggested in the interviews on how board members can develop confidence in the risk information they are provided are through the knowledge they have about the business and industry and by being part of a board with a diversity of skills and experiences.

Chapter 2

KNOW THE BUSINESS AND ITS INDUSTRY

Without a deep knowledge of the business and the industry, it is difficult for board members to assess the risk information provided to them. One board member stated what several others noted as well:

> You first have to understand the business, and that means to some degree understanding the industry. Once you do that you can sort of devise a sense for what the things are that adversely impact the company. Until you have a fair degree of appreciation of the businesses, it's almost impossible to know if you're getting the important risk information.

Gaining knowledge of the business by a board member requires "getting the numbers" and understanding them. A former chief financial officer (CFO) of several major organizations, now serving as a board member of three public organizations, recalled how, in his former role, he had to provide the numbers and now he'll "make everybody do it" when he serves on a board. He phrased it this way: "Here is a quarter we just finished and maybe we were sent something in advance [of the board meeting]. So, what I want is, as I go into the next quarter, I want you to tell me how we are going to do in the next quarter. How and why? And how is it going to get done?"

Continuing, this board member stated:

> So are we going to make a buck on earnings per share? And we're going to get half of it out of here with margins of this and prices of that and we're going to get 25 percent out of this business and Europe's going to carry me for this. That's how we are going to do it. Now, when we come back [to the next board meeting], I don't give a damn how we did versus prior year. All I want to know is how we did versus how you told us we were going to do. I want to know that they [management] understand the business. I want to know are they just lucky, which often they are. Or, do they really feel the business.

In such board deliberations, he continued, "You build up trust. They've got to give you everything you want [as a board member]. And I mean everything."

In a related story, this same director stated that at one of the organizations on whose board he serves, the board believed it did not get sufficient financial information. After some discussion with management, the information now provided to the board in advance of its meetings contains "an appendix in the back," so board members like him can explore it at will. This director emphasized that the CFO should know "every single page" in the appendix and be able to respond to questions by the board. While there are acceptable reasons for missing targets, a board, according to this individual, has to understand the numbers to assess the validity of the reasons for missing the targets. And as another board member noted, "You really have to understand the nuances of your business," and the "real work is two or three steps down into the data."

The point of trusting management and getting all the information you need from them to perform your oversight responsibilities was emphasized by another director in this way: "Your oversight is only as good as the data you are getting. There is no real independent way to get it. You can make sure you know the people, try to meet a lot of them.... Get a feel for what is going on and watch their body language, how they act around their superiors, what the mood is."

A suggestion was also made that a board member could gain knowledge about the business by attending the audit committee meeting even though he or she is not an official member. "It is important for all the board members to at least sit in on the audit committee meeting," observed one audit committee chair. The audit committee "is where you discuss everything. We end up discussing strategy — you have to." Unfortunately, in a number of the interviews, several board members noted that because various committees are meeting at the same time, it is often not possible to attend a committee meeting other than the one on which you are officially a member.

Another way for a board member to get to know the business and industry involves spending time understanding firsthand how the organization's products are viewed by customers. As an example, in the case of an organization with retail products, a board member said, "Once a month I get in my car and drive to Wal-Mart, Target, Walgreens, and other stores and look at our products and the shelf space."

This board member went on to say, "I start talking to the clerks, and I usually follow up with, 'Is this product a piece of crap or is it any good?' And I'll ask, 'What sells? Who has got some new gizmo here that is really selling well?'" With the information gained from his fieldwork, this board member does not hesitate to share what he has learned with his organization's management, even suggesting that they make a call to the retailer's home office, telling them, "We're not getting the shelf space that we're supposed to have."

The overall objective in gaining an understanding of the business and the industry is for a board member to develop his or her own independent business judgment about the organization. A board member explained:

> You have to be doing more work than just what the [management] is presenting. You have to read about competitors in the marketplace. You have to read analysts' reports. You have to read the research reports from the major research organizations, like Gartner and Forester. You have to make an effort to be informed yourself. It's not just showing up for the board meeting and reading what management gives you, which they think is right. They're not trying to give you something that is incorrect. You have to form an independent objective opinion.

In summarizing the role of the board, this same director stated:

> Your job is business judgment. That's what you are there to do, and you have to form your own independent business judgment based on what you've learned, what you've actively tried to understand, and part of what you do is you ask for presentations on materials that have a contrary and different view than the recommendation of management so you understand their logic and how they reached the conclusion. You just don't show up and say, "Oh, thank you for

the conclusion." You're supposed to know how they [management] reached the conclusion and what it is based on. That's what a meaningful board meeting covers.

A best practice is: **To assess and have confidence in the risk information provided by management, directors must have a thorough understanding of the business and industry.**

For CAEs and audit professionals: **1) Consider offering training to board members on the complexities of the business and the associated risk; 2) consider briefing notes for board members or pre-meetings with board members and/or committee chairs who have risk oversight responsibility; 3) recommend to those charged with risk oversight which risks or business units should be discussed; and 4) provide analysis or comparisons of risks disclosed by peer organizations.**

Chapter 3

BOARD MEMBERS' SKILLS AND EXPERIENCES

A second way for a board to gain confidence that it is receiving the right quantity and best quality of risk information from management is by having colleagues who collectively represent a diversified set of skills and experiences. Such a board can engage in robust discussions of the organization's ERM process and significant risks, thus enabling it to gain confidence in the risk information provided by management. These discussions may take place at the board level as well as in individual committees.

The important point is that, if there is not a diversity of skills and experiences represented on the board, its composition can be a risk factor. For an engineering and construction organizations, it does not mean you need only board members with that background. In fact, as a director observed, organizations "would not get the diversity of thought that you'd like under that scenario." Instead, you want board members with "different backgrounds, different interests, and different perspectives attempting to learn the business over a period of time from their perspective."

Another director commented that an individual board member must understand what their "perspective" is and what "they bring" to board deliberations. For example, this board member mentioned her background is in technology and, specifically, "go to market technology" and how "you use technology to be more competitive and to differentiate." From this particular board member's perspective, you want a board with "complementary and different perspectives." Otherwise, she observed, "If you and I see the world the same and have the same stigmatism, we're going to miss the same problems."

It is important to note the role of board committees and how a board with a diversity of skills and experiences adds value to its committees. One director described the role of committees:

> Board committees basically are formed and operated at the discretion of the board, and the purpose of committees is to help the board accomplish its overall objectives. Presumably the people who serve on committees do so because they have some special confidence in the areas that the committee is assigned to oversee, and the committee charters set forth the manner of what their responsibilities are.
>
> At the same time, if you have a failure in a committee, the fact that the committee has failed to some degree is a board failure. It means either you didn't have the right people on the committee, or it didn't have the right charter, scope of operation, or there was some sort of a failure in the execution of the committee.

In light of the new SEC risk oversight requirements, it is important for boards to update and recheck their committee charters to reflect risk responsibilities.[22]

Among the diversity of skills and experiences on a board, a question occasionally asked is: Should there be a board member who is designated as the risk expert for the board? Given the proliferation of risks that most organizations face, the notion of a single director designated as the so-called board's risk expert was viewed with some skepticism, as captured in this statement by a board member:

> I don't know who could be in our group as a risk expert because being on a board is sort of a team sport and various members bring various perspectives and backgrounds and knowledge on various issues.... Saying that one person has superior ability to assess all the risks that our company has, I don't think that our board would agree with that as there are just too many risks.

In contrast, Senator Schumer has proposed risk committees and the Dodd-Frank Act mandates risk committees and board risk experts. Additionally, the National Association of Corporate Directors (NACD) lists "risk management" expertise as a skill choice for members. One board member noted that they are seeking ERM and risk governance board members.

A critical question is, even with the diversity of board member skills and experiences, can a board be absolutely comfortable that management has identified all the organization's risk? In addressing this question, a board member candidly pointed out that a healthy skepticism is still needed by directors regarding the risks facing the organization:

> I don't think we are comfortable.... I think the biggest fear you have is that there are some material risks out there that you didn't foresee and that you weren't monitoring that you should have been.... Again, if you understand the businesses you have and understand the industries, it becomes easier to get comfortable that you're catching the main ones.... But at the same time, what you fear is that what will bite you is what you didn't see.

Another board member was a little more direct in response to this question, stating, "I think anybody who says that they are completely satisfied is arrogant."

A best practice is: **Compose the board's membership so that it has the diversity of skills and experiences necessary to fulfill its risk oversight responsibilities. Boards should continually assess their own talents and skills related to risk management and risk oversight.**

For CAEs and audit professionals: **1) Be aware of board members' backgrounds and skills; 2) be available to offer risk training; and 3) be ready and available to the board to provide an independent perspective on the business(es) risks and risk management processes.**

Chapter 4

DOCUMENTING BOARD RISK OVERSIGHT

When the board receives a report on the significant risks of the organization, an issue is: How will the board use the diverse skills and experiences of its members to provide risk oversight? It is not uncommon to assign the audit committee directly with the oversight responsibilities for the majority of the risks. In a Public Company Governance Survey conducted by the NACD in 2008, audit committees were assigned the oversight responsibilities for 67 percent of the risks.[23] However, it is not unusual for the audit committee, by referring to the board committee charters, to assign the oversight over specific risks to appropriate committees. The full board has oversight responsibility for strategic risks.

In some cases, two committees may share the lead for oversight of a significant risk. As an example, an area of overlap may occur where the audit committee has responsibility for compliance risk with regard to financial reporting, but the health, safety, and environmental committee (HSE) has "full oversight responsibilities with respect to safety of the company's employees." In this situation, the HSE committee is expected "to lead the way in terms of what type of safety standards" the organization has, and as a board member stated, "Quite frankly, in many instances, the safety standards we have for projects we work on are much higher than what the law requires."

Figure 1 illustrates how a board's risk oversight responsibilities can be shared among its committees. Using this diagram, along with an assumed set of board committee charters and an assumed list of major risks, Figure 1 shows which committees take the lead in oversight for the 17 risks based on the charters. For some risks, two committees share the lead responsibilities.

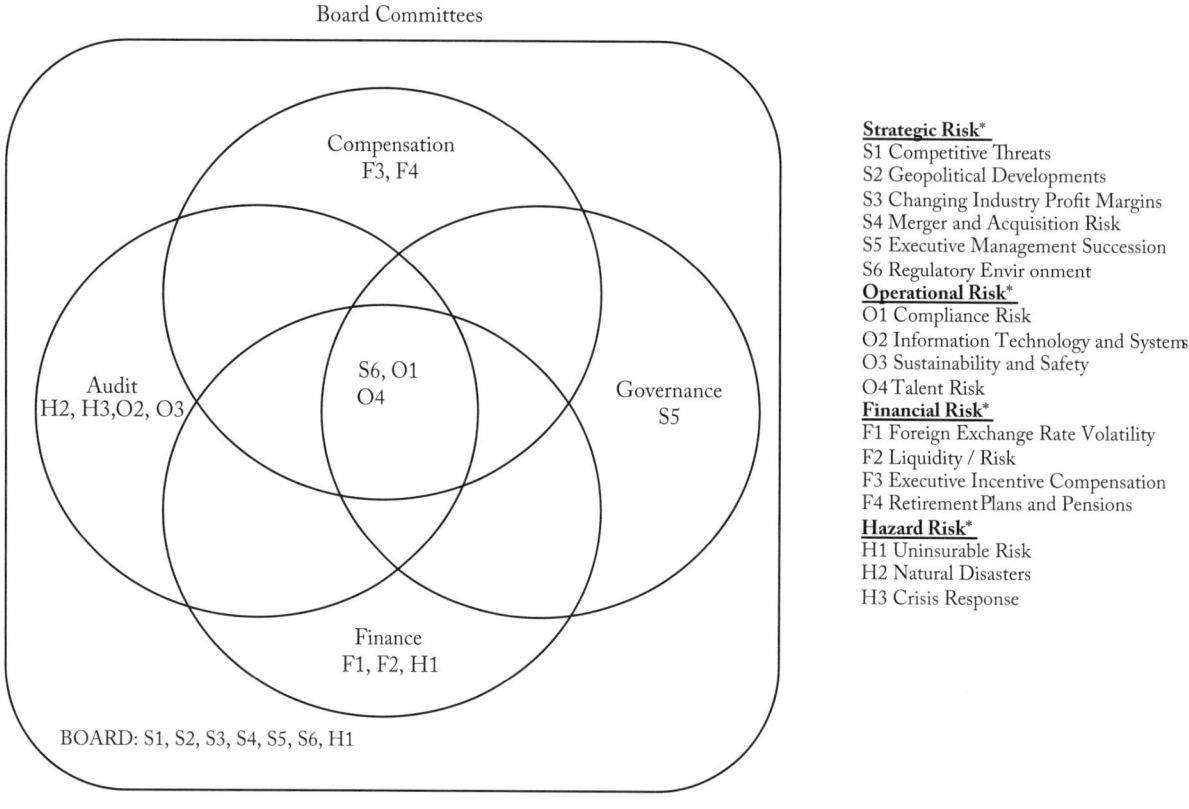

Figure 1: Board Committee Risk Assignments

Board Committees

- Compensation: F3, F4
- Audit: H2, H3, O2, O3
- Governance: S5
- Finance: F1, F2, H1
- Center (overlap): S6, O1, O4
- BOARD: S1, S2, S3, S4, S5, S6, H1

Strategic Risk*
S1 Competitive Threats
S2 Geopolitical Developments
S3 Changing Industry Profit Margins
S4 Merger and Acquisition Risk
S5 Executive Management Succession
S6 Regulatory Environment

Operational Risk*
O1 Compliance Risk
O2 Information Technology and Systems
O3 Sustainability and Safety
O4 Talent Risk

Financial Risk*
F1 Foreign Exchange Rate Volatility
F2 Liquidity / Risk
F3 Executive Incentive Compensation
F4 Retirement Plans and Pensions

Hazard Risk*
H1 Uninsurable Risk
H2 Natural Disasters
H3 Crisis Response

*This risk framework was used in: Paul L. Walker, William G. Shenkir, & Thomas L. Barton, *Enterprise Risk Management: Pulling it All Together*, (Altamonte Springs, Fl: Institute of Internal Auditors Research Foundation, 2002), p.5.

Another way to document board risk oversight, in addition to other critical information about each of the significant risks, is in a Risk Management Alignment Guide (see Figure 2).[24] This guide indicates for each significant risk the risk owner, any risk appetite metric, processes for monitoring the risk, action plans to improve risk oversight, executive responsibility for the risk, and board risk oversight, whether the full board or a specific board committee. This report provides a concise summary to communicate the "organization's overall risk management practices."[25]

Figure 2: Risk Management Alignment Guide Example*

Risk Category	Risk Owner(s)	Risk Appetite Metrics	Monitoring	Action Plans	Company Oversight	Board Oversight
Reputation Risk	CEO	Policy, Including Specific Metrics, Approved xx/xx/xx.	Corporate Communications.	Approved and Updated xx/xx/xx.	Executive Committee	Full Board
Operations Risk	COO	Daily Operations Metrics in Place in All Operating Divisions.	Operations Management Daily Monitoring and Reporting.	Plans in Place for Each Trigger Point.	Risk Management Internal Audit	Risk Committee
Information Technology Risk	CTO	Policies, Including Daily Performance Metrics, in Place for Security, Backup, and Recovery.	Daily Monitoring Against Established Performance Standards.	Contingency and Backup Plans in Place and Periodically Tested.	Operating Committee Internal Audit	Audit Committee Full Board

*Source: Mark L. Frigo and Richard J. Anderson, *"Embracing Enterprise Risk Management: Practical Approaches for Getting Started"* (COSO, 2011).

A best practice is: **A board should have a process to assure that all the risks identified are appropriately assigned to the various committees for oversight responsibility. The audit committee can serve as the lead committee that assigns risks for oversight to various board committees or to the full board, which should retain oversight for strategic risks.**

For CAEs and audit professionals: **1) Provide an annual assessment of the ERM process; 2) provide an assessment of the effectiveness of management's response to the risks; 3) test the effectiveness of related risk mitigation controls; 4) provide assurance that the risk oversight structure is appropriate; and 5) provide recommendations or best practices to assist in enhancing the risk management process.**

Chapter 5

STRATEGY, STRATEGIC RISK, AND ERM

The two activities of strategy setting and ERM can be viewed as "two sides of the same coin." A director offered this perspective: "To me one of the critical things that has to take place, and I question whether it takes place in a lot of corporations, but there's got to be a very, very tight linkage between the strategic planning process and the risk management process." This director explains:

> These two exercises have to be linked. If not, you have the people that are doing the strategic planning without real focus. They're not really focused on how they're going to manage the risks of the changes that are going to take place in the business. By the same token, the people who are looking at these risks need to be looking over the horizon to see what kind of risks we're going to be dealing with a year from now or five years from now.

In 2004, the Committee of Sponsoring Organizations of the Treadway Commission (COSO) published *Enterprise Risk Management – Integrated Framework* and recognized this linkage, stating that ERM is a process "applied in strategy setting" and "across the enterprise."[26] Similarly, the International Organization for Standardization (ISO) 31000 Standard issued in 2009 recognized that risk management should be embedded in "business and strategic planning and review."[27] Organizations make a mistake when they fail to link strategy and risk management because "a strategy that lacks alignment to risk management is not only insufficient but downright dangerous."[28] Furthermore, "risk management is pointless unless it is closely tied to the company's strategic objectives."[29]

The importance of linking strategy setting and risk management was documented in a Booz Allen Hamilton study. According to this study, from 1999 through 2003, the primary events causing organizations to lose shareholder value were strategic and operational failures. This study analyzed 1,200 firms whose market capitalization exceeded US $1 billion. The 360 worst performing firms suffered losses of which 87 percent could be attributed to strategic and operational mismanagement.[30] Another study by Mercer Management Consulting analyzed the value collapses in the Fortune 1000 from 1993 to 1998. This study found that 10 percent of the Fortune 1000 lost 25 percent of shareholder value within one month. Tracing the loss to the root causes revealed that 58 percent of the losses were the result of strategic risks and 31 percent by operating risks.[31]

Both of these studies indicate that when the board and management are considering strategic alternatives, they need to know as much as they can about the risks embedded in the various options. One board member said, "You go through the strategy or the alternate strategy and look at the risk associated" with each option. The potential impact of strategic risks was captured by one director who described them as the "risks that could take the company down," and by another one who observed, "When you start looking at strategic risks, you're looking at freight trains and not box cars." In thinking about strategic risks, a director who had served on approximately 25 boards over the years offered this insight: "From the risk oversight point of view, the biggest vulnerability is when you have a lot of change in your business model and when you are rapidly growing."

An audit committee chair described how they linked strategy setting and ERM in his organization. They formed a team composed of the CEO, CFO, CAE, board chair of the governance committee, and himself to design a program for integrating strategic planning and ERM, which works as follows:

> As we're going through our annual strategic planning process (which we do in the summer) and present to the board of directors our strategic plan and set of strategic issues in a September meeting, we will, concurrently with that, do our risk assessment. So the risk is looked at in light of the strategy, and the solutions to risk issues will be embedded in the resource allocation processes of the company.

For the strategy meeting of the board in September, the directors receive an enterprise risk assessment in "a book about 40 or 50 pages long which identifies the top 40 or 50 risks that management identified — where they were last year, are they new, what's happened, what's changed and when did they change, and anything new that's come up." As they began this process several years ago, "each of the risks was assigned to an officer of the company and, in that section of the presentation, they would talk about the top risks that they saw in their area and what they were doing to mitigate them. And we did that concurrent with the strategic plan."

The linkage of strategy setting and risk management is enhanced by dual appointments of a director to both the board's strategic planning committee and audit committee. A director, who chairs the audit committee, explains, "We have a strategic planning committee, which a member of the audit committee chairs, and also the chair of the strategic planning committee is probably my most effective member on the audit committee. And I sit on the strategic planning committee also." The dual appointments have, according to this audit committee chair, led to a more robust strategic planning process as well as a robust risk management process.

Implementing ERM led a director to assert, "ERM helped us put our strategy together." To explain, the CEO has "got to report to us on his strategy every quarter anyway. Where we are. And we don't set strategy and put the plan in the bottom drawer. There is a quarterly check off on execution of strategy. So having that is also part of your ERM."

Along this same line of thinking, a director pointed out that they "use ERM to really understand" the business and "turn that into a competitive advantage" and "open stores more quickly than competitors." As an example, ERM revealed that they had a lack of diversity in their stores and now they have a "strategy of diversification." In another organization, a director felt "the awareness that the ERM process" has brought to the board and senior management probably made them "a lot smarter" in looking at a recent acquisition than they "might have been otherwise."

As noted in Figure 1, a best practice is: **Assign to the entire board the responsibility for risk oversight of strategic risks as part of its strategy-planning deliberations.**

For CAEs and audit professionals: **1) Provide a review or assessment of the risk responsibility assignments; 2) provide an assessment of the strategic risk management process, including performance measurement practices; and 3) provide an independent analysis or assessment of the organization's strategic risks.**

Chapter 6

INDICATING RISK VELOCITY ON A RISK MAP

The risk information provided to a board usually includes a risk map where the major risks of the organization are plotted according to impact and likelihood (probability). Using these two dimensions, the task is to determine the probability that a risk event will occur, and if it does, what the dollar impact will be. The metric for dollar impact varies, but some that are used include revenue, net operating profit, or earnings per share.

With a proliferation of risks confronting organizations, coupled with a rapidly changing business environment, adding risk velocity to a risk map provides very useful information. Risk velocity attempts to assess how quickly a given risk will move from occurrence of the event to its impact. By using a specified nomenclature, risk velocity can be incorporated on a risk map where each risk is noted with a special mark or color indicating how fast the impact will occur once the risk event takes place.

A CAE of an organization that had been implementing ERM for more than a decade pointed out in the interview that until 2008 they had not incorporated velocity in their risk management process. However, the CAE noted that when the global crisis of 2008 hit, they found:

> What was theoretical became real. And it became real very fast. What we learned was that we had not considered velocity. We had all of these heat maps and fancy charts and mitigating discussions and great meetings but when grain prices went through the roof, when energy prices went through the roof, what was a theoretical exercise became real.
>
> I think management felt we didn't act quickly enough and we didn't really incorporate velocity into our risk management process. So you've identified all of these risks and you could say, "OK, low likelihood, high impact," and you spotted it on this fancy chart and it looked great, but there was missing how quickly could this thing happen. So that was a key learning that you have to look at velocity.

To illustrate velocity, in Figure 1, regulatory environment is listed as a strategic risk, and liquidity risk is identified as a financial risk. Consider the following assessment of these two risks:

> Both can put you out of business. But regulatory risk develops relatively slowly. You get a notice from a regulator, have time to respond, and even in the worst case where there may be criminal sanctions, you have time to prepare a defense. In contrast, liquidity risk manifests quickly. Within a week or two, your counterparties stop dealing with you and you're out of business.[32]

In monitoring risks, an understanding of "how quickly a risk metastasizes into impact"[33] is essential if an organization is going to develop an effective response plan. In presenting a risk map to the board, management can indicate the velocity for the risks on the heat map. As an example, through special marks and/or colors, the velocity of each risk on a map can be graded as very rapid for impact evident within a month, rapid for impact evident in a quarter, or slow for impact evident in a year.[34] Also, a report to the board can list the top five risks by likelihood, impact, and velocity.

A best practice is: **Include in a heat map provided to the board an assessment of the velocity of each risk, and consider providing a report listing for each of the significant risks' impact, likelihood, and velocity.**

For CAEs and audit professionals: **1) Know and be ready to provide assessment of the velocity of major risks; and 2) review the risk dashboards and risk heat maps to confirm the velocity assigned to each major risk.**

Chapter 7

ERM TRAINING FOR THE BOARD AND MANAGEMENT

Training board members on the fundamentals of ERM — risk identification, risk assessment, risk response, and monitoring — is imperative. As one director pointed out, "You think you know something about risk management." However, if you want "to formalize the process" in an organization, you need training. He explained:

> When I started looking at this [ERM] five years ago when it got really hot, I basically went to the Corporate Executive Board. They do a lot of best practice studies. And then I went to the various auditing firms and gathered who does ERM, who does it well, and what are the risks? I sort of chased it down for about a year going to various meetings, seminars, and sessions.

This director continued:

> I think the conclusion that I got out of it pretty early on was that 80+ percent of the risks to companies are operational and strategic. They're not regulatory or financial. And, therefore, a purely regulatory or financial risk management program, particularly in an operating company as opposed to a bank, is a relatively shallow look at the real set of issues.

With training, this director served as a member of a committee that developed a program linking the strategic planning process and ERM.

At another organization, a director reflecting on the risk management process indicated that initially they were focused on financial risks, and the internal auditor headed up the effort. The board decided that they "weren't doing enough" in risk management so they "sat down with management" and asked the audit committee chair to "monitor" a process, saying, "Let's see if we can't get some depth here." They appointed a chief risk officer (CRO) who "went to a lot of classes, came back and shared structure" with the audit committee chair. Meanwhile, the chair "was talking to CFOs and other board members." He asked them, "What are you doing [in risk management]?" That was the process they used to educate themselves on ERM and strengthen the organization's risk management process.

Other directors who were interviewed mentioned that they had risk consultants present to the board on ERM at one of their regular meetings or at a board retreat. In addition, directors noted that they had, on their own initiative, attended ERM conferences and seminars. One director highlighted their training approach: "We've made everybody get educated. There have been a lot of outside speakers come in and talk to us about risk management." One board also made sure the CRO knew what they were doing and held them accountable: "We sent our ERM guy to conferences. He went to four conferences. He sent me notes when he came back, looking for models, …seeing what other people are doing."

A best practice is: **The board and individual directors should assess their ERM knowledge and determine what training and education are needed to be able to perform risk oversight responsibilities.**

For CAEs and audit professionals: **1) Stay current on ERM tools, techniques, and best practices; 2) benchmark and network with peer groups on risk practices; 3) provide a briefing of ERM and risk oversight best practices to those charged with risk oversight; and 4) identify conferences or programs on risk practices that would be appropriate for the organization's directors or executives.**

Chapter 8

SCANNING AND RECALIBRATION OF RISKS

The business world has probably never been exposed to change as rapidly as we are witnessing today. The expansion of global business and improvements in communication are important reasons for this increased speed of change. A risk that an organization considers to be critical today might be tagged as merely a blip two years from now. Likewise, a risk may be off the radar today but rise to the top within that same two years.

This corporate fact of life has important implications for the operation of an ERM system. A static, check-the-box ERM system is doomed to be mired in the past and unable to cope with new risks that appear suddenly. Old risks that have lost significance consume resources and distract attention away from newer, unmanaged risks if they remain at their original position in the map of critical risks.

Because technological innovation is the root of much of the change in the business environment, examples from a large multinational technology company seem particularly appropriate. It was well documented, for instance, that Microsoft, basically a software company, encountered serious reliability problems with its Xbox video game console.

Microsoft launched the Xbox in 2001 and positioned it to compete with the PlayStation 2 from Sony and the GameCube from Nintendo. This was Microsoft's first attempt at competing at the hardware level with industry leaders Sony and Nintendo, both well entrenched in high-end gaming systems. A later product, the Xbox 360, exhibited serious reliability problems, and Microsoft launched a very costly extended warranty program, described as follows in its 2007 10-K:

> In July 2007, we expanded our global Xbox 360 warranty coverage to three years from the date of purchase for a general hardware failure indicated by three flashing red lights. As a result, we recorded a $1.06 billion charge for anticipated costs under the warranty policy, inventory write-downs, and product returns.[35]

One would expect the Xbox 360 situation to represent substantial risk to Microsoft, and the company candidly acknowledges this in Item 1A, Risk Factors in its 2007 10-K:

> **Our consumer hardware products may experience quality or supply problems.** Our hardware products such as the Xbox 360 console are highly complex and can have defects in design, manufacture, or associated software. We could incur significant expenses, lost revenue, and reputational harm if we fail to detect or effectively address such issues through design, testing, or warranty repairs.[36]

Microsoft's rapid and effective response to the Xbox 360 risk would naturally lead to that risk becoming less important over time. Concurrently, the rise of cloud computing, in which customer business information is stored on remote servers managed by Microsoft, creates a whole new set of risks to be identified and controlled.[37] In this era of sophisticated hackers, the possibility of sensitive corporate information being compromised is a real threat with a very high level of cost, direct and indirect, attached if it happens.[38]

Cloud computing for Microsoft is an example of an emerging risk. Time is of the essence in capturing emerging risks in an ERM system. A company stands a much better chance of managing an unexpected negative event effectively if the risk has already been identified and the company is prepared to deal with it when, or if, it actually occurs. The CAE of a major retailer gives this example:

> We also have a list of emerging risks. And this is much more of a dynamic list — there are many more changes to this list than there are for the top 10 [risks]. We look for emerging risks in the retail space and, of course, in the industry in general and just the environment in general.

For this company, the search for emerging risks resulted in the identification of a new federal regulation that, if passed, would dramatically alter the company's business model. Most importantly, it would alter the wage scale and reduce the number of employees the company could afford to hire. Given that this company has a heavy emphasis on high-quality customer service, it was very beneficial for the risk to be identified as early as possible.

Anticipating potential problems can yield powerful competitive advantages. A board member of a heavily regulated company had this to say:

> It's the things you don't plan for that are going to get you. You never expect it, but I can tell you the things that have happened to us [in a regulatory action] were pretty dire when you think about the financial effect on the market value. [But] we anticipated these [in the current situation involving regulatory approval]. We think we'll get approval [in the first round], we may not at the panel [second round]. What are we going to do if we don't? Why would they not approve us? What would it be? Well, we went through those issues and we were ready to respond.

Accompanying the rapid change in technology facing businesses is the need for the firm's business model to adapt to changes in the micro and macro environments. A company and its board that sit back and bask in the status quo are headed for trouble. It is absolutely critical that management and the board maintain an awareness of their ever-changing risk portfolio. A board member makes this observation: "I think that from the risk oversight point of view, the biggest vulnerability is when you have a lot of change to your business model."

How is the business model changing? New systems? Shifted more overseas? Made acquisitions? New financing? Succession planning? These all change the risk portfolio. Management and boards must understand their business model, and that includes understanding the competition.

A board member of a high-growth technology company said:

> Our strategic business risks are enormous. The one that we do a constant, detailed review on is the competitive risk. One of our direct competitors got acquired by a large company. How do we compete against a company that is 15 times bigger than us, who has market power, who's a

bully? And who could under-price and decide to hammer down the profit margin just to kill us, as a business strategy? So we talk about those kinds of risks.

In this situation, the CEO himself was a strategic risk because the board thought he did not have the right skills and ideas to compete with the bigger rival. He was replaced, but this created a new risk: Will his successor do better and will the team accept his vision?

It is certainly a daunting task for a board to ensure that changing or emerging risks are adequately considered in the ERM program. The stakes are very high and even potentially ruinous for ill-prepared companies. Consider the prominent brands in technology from an earlier era that don't even exist today: Borland, Lotus, WordStar, and many others. So how is a board to know if changing or emerging risks are being covered? Probably the best solution is for board members to be experts on their own companies — to understand the company's industry, competition, and challenges. This allows them to ask the right questions and determine whether the answers are reasonable. A board member states, "My own view is, if the board understands the company, understands the company's strategy, understands what's happening in the company, risks really ought not to be something where you form a special committee at the board level to see what is going on as [Big Bank] did."

Recently, one individual received the same basic email from five different major online retailers:

> Dear Valued Customer,
>
> On [date], we were informed by [Company X], a company we use to send emails to our customers, that files containing the email addresses of some [Retailer] customers were accessed without authorization.
>
> We have been assured by [Company X] that the only information that was obtained was your email address. No other personally identifiable information was at risk because such data is not contained in [Company X]'s email system.
>
> For your security, we encourage you to be aware of common email scams that ask for personal or sensitive information. [Retailer] will not send you emails asking for your credit card number, Social Security number, or other personally identifiable information. If ever asked for this information, you can be confident it is not from [Retailer].
>
> We regret this has taken place and any inconvenience this may have caused you. If you have any questions regarding this issue, please contact us at [toll free number]. We take your privacy very seriously, and we will continue to work diligently to protect your personal information.
>
> Sincerely,
>
> Customer Service Team

Technology represents one of the biggest sources of emerging risk for companies today. It is likely that Company X represented to the retailers that its information was secure, yet it was clearly not. This security lapse is a potentially costly matter for the retailers but could be catastrophic for Company X. In this technology era, firms should expect that emerging risks can hit quickly and hit hard. (We covered the related topic of velocity in a previous section.)

It is impossible for the board to be seers, to anticipate and prepare for all serious eventualities. A formal ERM process is a good step, but nothing is perfect. As a board member observed, "I think anybody that says that they are completely satisfied [that all risks have been identified] is arrogant."

To summarize: **Because of a rapidly evolving landscape, some risks drop in importance quickly and others rise to the top tier in record time. Some even come from out of nowhere. A best practice in risk identification, then, is to scan the environment often and critically, prioritize the recalibration of the top tier risk set, and have a mechanism in place to evaluate and incorporate important emerging risks into the system.**

For CAEs and audit professionals: **1) Provide a periodic assessment or updates of the emerging risks; 2) stay informed of developments related to the industry and business model that could alter the organization's risk profile; and 3) serve as a catalyst to prompt ongoing discussions with a management working group or committee to discuss emerging risks.**

Chapter 9

RISK REPORTING

One of the most critical areas of ERM oversight by the board is risk reporting, or the mechanism by which the board learns of critical risks, plans to mitigate them, and the performance of management in meeting the risk objectives. Boards have only very limited opportunities to view the ERM process directly. After all, the board doesn't actually manage the risks — that's the job of company management. Board members rely on management to inform them periodically about the process, and issues of information accuracy, timeliness, and relevance come into play. While the board does not manage the risks, it is responsible for ensuring that the risks are, in fact, being managed — and being managed effectively.

So the risk communication between management and the board — the risk reporting mechanism — must yield high-quality information. For instance, if a company has a massive, highly risky derivative exposure, but the risk reports, for whatever reason, paint a picture of only moderate risk exposure, the board might be lulled into a false sense of security that would last until the derivative position exploded. Quite simply, effective board oversight of risk is impossible without sound risk reporting. Best practices in this area can often be achieved with a modest investment of resources — that's not the problem. It's evaluating the process realistically and ensuring that it is effective *before* a risk debacle happens, not *after*. "Learning the hard way" in risk oversight is inefficient at best and downright dangerous or catastrophic at worst.

We found that best practices companies, as would be expected, employ a variety of risk reporting approaches tailored to their specific characteristics, structures, and needs. An organization with a board risk committee would have one approach, and an organization that works through its audit committee would have another approach. The best practice is not the committee structure itself; it is the specifics of how the risk reporting framework informs the board members about the management of the risks. No one will notice the committee structure if a risk exposure blows up. Instead, the focus will be on why the board didn't know about the severity of the situation beforehand and have the opportunity to ensure it would be mitigated timely. That is a risk reporting issue — and a serious one.

It is often helpful to refer back to authoritative risk standards for guidance. ISO 31000 addresses risk reporting, primarily in Section 4.3.6, "Establishing internal communications and reporting mechanisms." ISO 31000 is a framework and, as such, does not directly promulgate best practices. The standards can and should shape the best practices themselves. But there could even be several best practices for a given standard. Sections 4.3.6 and a related section, A.3.4 (Annex, or Appendix A), appear below:

4.3.6 Establishing internal communication and reporting mechanisms

The organization should establish internal communication and reporting mechanisms in order to support and encourage accountability and ownership of risk. These mechanisms should ensure that:

- key components of the risk management framework, and any subsequent modifications, are communicated appropriately;
- there is adequate internal reporting on the framework, its effectiveness and the outcomes;
- relevant information derived from the application of risk management is available at appropriate levels and times; and
- there are processes for consultation with internal stakeholders.

These mechanisms should, where appropriate, include processes to consolidate risk information from a variety of sources, and may need to consider the sensitivity of the information.[39]

A.3.4 Continual communications

Enhanced risk management includes continual communications with external and internal stakeholders, including comprehensive and frequent reporting of risk management performance, as part of good governance.

This can be indicated by communication with stakeholders as an integral and essential component of risk management. Communication is rightly seen as a two-way process, such that properly informed decisions can be made about the level of risks and the need for risk treatment against properly established and comprehensive risk criteria.

Comprehensive and frequent external and internal reporting on both significant risks and on risk management performance contributes substantially to effective governance within an organization.[40]

Best practices in board risk reporting are shaped by the level of integration of risk awareness and control already embedded in the company and its operations. It has been said many times that effective ERM is woven into the company's culture and becomes an almost automatic process. If this is the case in a given company — and it should be — risk reporting is considerably simplified. The best practices discussed here assume that such a cultural integration exists. Effective ERM demands that consideration of risk at the board level be an extension of a risk program already in place, not merely an additional task for board members to tackle at their quarterly meetings.

The CAE of a major retailer put it this way:

> We have very strong risk management embedded in the company, and that's where I think ERM belongs. I think if your board has a lot of faith in your CEO and his or her direct reports, and they know that the company manages risk really well, this shouldn't be a separate exercise. I mean, risk should be discussed all the time in the boardroom.

In some ways, there are natural barriers to effective board risk reporting. One is the reluctance of some CEOs to share reliable risk information with the board. It is not the existence of the risks that is at issue here — competent board members should already know what the key risks are. Rather, it's the relative severity of the risks and, perhaps even more importantly, the level to which management is effectively managing the risks. No CEO wants to be put in the position of saying, "Our derivative exposure is a huge risk and, unfortunately, we're doing a poor job of managing it." It's more likely the CEO would be inclined to say that the company is "on top" of the derivative exposure and does not expect any significant losses. Board members must be vigilant about such "happy talk."

Consider also an internal auditor who is leery of sharing "too much" risk information with the board for fear of being audited himself — having the information challenged and picked apart. In such cases, the culture of the organization has the effect of "shutting down" the reporting lines. One board member said, "Everyone is wired to try to avoid."

Risk reporting to the board is potentially a huge task and board members can get overloaded with information, while managers can get complacent about risks, believing, or wanting to believe, that all the risks are being managed. A board member proposed this solution: "I'd say the biggest trick in all of these kinds of routine processes is you've got to keep it fresh so people don't just go through the steps and not really do the work. Today, the board gets the [ERM] book ahead of time that shows what's changed, what hasn't changed, on the list and why. Keeping the process fresh and sharp becomes the role of the board — by keeping an active dialog on the big risks."

Another natural barrier to effective board risk reporting is a tendency to report infrequently, say annually. This is actually linked to a CEO's "happy face" view of risk reporting — "We're doing well in our risk management, so why do we need to report on it all the time?" But as they become more informed and risk-aware, boards tend to want the information more frequently. One audit executive said, "Every single one of them [on his audit committee, which is involved in risk] said, you know, we really want to see those top 10 lists quarterly, which has really probably become a best practice now."

But the most in-depth risk reporting is normally done less frequently. For instance, a board member describes the process in one of his companies:

> Every strategy meeting in September – formally for the first couple of years; now, less formally — we get a report ... which identifies the top 40 or 50 risks that management identified — where they were last year, are they new, what's happened, what's changed and when did they change and anything new that's come up. Each of the risks was assigned to an officer of the company and in that section of the strategic presentation, they would talk about the top risks that they saw in their area and what they were doing to mitigate them.

As to the number of risks typically reported to the board, organizations varied from five up to 50. The norm, though, seems to be between 10 and 20 risks. Given that the board is limited to risk oversight, it would appear that routinely reporting on 50 risks is perhaps too much for boards to digest effectively. If the board risk reporting is reliable, one would expect that reporting on 10 to 20 risks would be sufficient. In support of this notion, one board member stated pithily, "All boards ask companies to explain the biggest risks. If they don't, then they are a really bad board."

The issue of looking to a committee instead of the entire board for risk oversight is an important one. Initially, it seemed that boards tended to delegate the oversight to committees, typically the audit committee or perhaps a separate risk committee. Then that designated committee would report to the entire board. In some companies, meetings were scheduled so that all board members could sit in on these "risk meetings." There is some evidence that change is taking place in communicating risk information to the board. This is from a CAE:

> Once a year I do a deep dive into ERM to just update them [the board members] on how we do what we do. It's a formal agenda item that's discussed in depth. This year will be the first year I'm actually doing it to the full board. So, while in the past the audit committee has had the responsibility of governing risk management for [our company] and then reporting to the full board about what they do in their meetings, I'm now going to do the deep dive to the full board, not just to the audit committee, which I think will be a good practice moving forward. So you can see that it's evolving.

A similar observation comes from an audit committee chair: "The board decided we weren't doing enough depth [with the current ERM approach]. That's when they decided the new CRO should report to the whole board and not just the audit committee." In this case, the CRO has a line directly to the entire board.

The risk reporting need not be overly complicated to be effective. It is important to remember that the board is not actually managing the risks — it is exercising oversight. One board member explains: "What we did was just adopt the matrix that I think nine out of 10 companies have, which is how severe is the risk and what is the likelihood of it happening? You know that sort of nine-box matrix that everybody uses and color codes. And we basically accepted that and ran with that as the issue."

The informativeness of the reporting is key. One board member grades the presentation to the board not based on the risk maps but how well the risks were communicated to the board audience.

> We have a risk committee of the board and they do an annual assessment of the risks. Then they have an internal committee above that that drills down very deeply and decides, OK, what really are the enterprise risks? Those are shared with the board in depth annually after they finish their assessment. And then we get quarterly updates.
>
> So we've got red, yellow, and green lights from a dashboard presented at the board meeting. We grouped the risks into five groups — economy, strategy, legal, corporate, and kind of business and operation risk. So you have a trend and a risk level assessment of each of those five bigger buckets. Underneath them are a lot of smaller buckets.

In 2009, the U.S. Securities and Exchange Commission (SEC) issued Final Rule 33-9089, "Proxy Disclosure Enhancements," which became effective in late February 2010. The rule directly impacts risk reporting issues. An important component of the rule was a requirement that companies document the relationship between management and the board in risk oversight. While the rule was not prescriptive, there was strong indication that the SEC expected companies to have effective risk oversight mechanisms and that the details of the mechanisms be readily available to stakeholders. Board members should review the company's risk oversight disclosures to ensure they are consistent with the practices and processes that are in place.

In Barton, Shenkir, and Walker [2010], the authors recommended that companies be motivated by the SEC rule to accomplish:

- Improving communication between board committees. Under the current environment, it is possible that each committee knows some risks but does not see the big picture. Boards need to connect the risk dots.

- Updating the charter of the committee(s) that takes responsibility for risk (many companies currently only have vague comments on risk and frequently they only refer to internal control related risks — not the same idea of risk that the SEC is pursuing in this rule).[41]

A major concern of the SEC is that board risk oversight be independent of the actual management of risk. This is akin to the old concern about an auditor auditing his own work. Some boards emphasize this independence idea by having risk conversations without the CEO present. According to one board member, "The CEO's in there for half of that but he's not in there for the other half." If one person is both the CEO and chairman, one recommendation is altering the charter for the lead director and the governance committee to increase the areas of review.

A best practice for board risk reporting is: **The reporting system should be tailored to the needs of the organization and exhibit the following characteristics:**

- **Reporting is sufficiently detailed to allow the board members to recognize and understand the key risks facing the organization and interconnectedness. Identifying five to 20 key risks seems optimal; some organizations elect to report on more.**

- **Reporting is routine and occurs frequently.**

- **Reporting includes updates on the status of management action plans related to key risks.**

- **Although primary reporting should be to the designated committees or individual directors, every director receives informative risk reports.**

- **Directors are trained to understand the organization's key risks and the management of them. For some directors, this will necessitate training in ERM generally.**

- **Risk oversight is independent of the organization's CEO, but the CEO is part of the risk-management dialog. Risk reporting is direct to the board members without filtering, scrubbing, or diluting.**

- **The entire reporting process is iterative. Information flows both ways — to the board and from the board in the form of feedback on the actual risk management and the quality of the reporting itself.**

For CAEs and audit professionals: **1) Review the organization's current risk reporting for completeness, timeliness, accuracy, and relevance; 2) compare the organization's reporting to the board best practices listed above; 3) if possible, assist with the deep dive into the risks; 4) consider whether the "tone at the top" of the organization has negatively impacted risk reporting; 5) review the organization's proxy risk oversight disclosures as well as its 10-K risk factor disclosures; 6) compare risk disclosures to peer organizations; and 7) discuss with the external auditors their assessment of the organization's risks.**

Chapter 10

ERM PROCESS

An organization's actual ERM process is shaped by many factors — corporate culture and traditions, organizational leadership, resource allocation, and board structure, among others. The result is there can be strong, effective ERM systems with widely differing characteristics. In some ways, this is a bit troublesome. It would seem desirable that there be a degree of standardization in best practices. In reality, good ERM systems differ among themselves significantly in process, and companies are satisfied with the results, which is the ultimate test.

While it is difficult to find a company in which the internal audit department is *not* a significant part of the ERM structure, the role of the internal auditors in the ERM process varies widely. In the best practices companies we examined, the responsibility of the internal audit unit varied from "in-charge" to "advisory." It must be emphasized that it is *not* a best practice for internal auditors to actually own the risks themselves, but a best practice could include internal auditors as key participants in the ERM process as long as proper safeguards are in place. For more detail, see Figure 4: Roles the Internal Auditor Can Do, Can Do with Safeguards, and Cannot Do with Respect to Risk Management. Organizations should not forget that risk management is basically a management function, while internal audit is an assurance and consultative function.

As ERM systems mature over time, it should be expected that the role of the internal audit unit will evolve from advisory to more of an assurance function. Of course, the specific role of the internal auditor in ERM is a conscious decision the board must make, with input from the CAE. After due consideration, some boards may want to mix the internal auditor's assurance and advisory roles.

No matter their role in the organization, CAEs are intimately familiar with their ERM processes and their evolution. Even mature and successful ERM systems[42] have evolved over time as organizations fine-tune their efforts to maximize the value. Sometimes ERM is really an evolution from previous risk management activities that had been uncoordinated but generally successful.

The CAE of a major retailer describes the company's realization that ERM was a distinct improvement over its previous risk management efforts:

> We actually started down this journey back in 2006 after [Sarbanes-Oxley] was sort of embedded [in our company], and a lot of the accounting firms and consulting firms were going around talking about ERM. And, quite frankly, I think a lot of them thought it was the second coming of [Sarbanes-Oxley] in terms of their next big revenue generator.
>
> And they were really selling this: You need to have this massive structure in place, and you need to be doing all of these things. And so one of the things I try to do a lot is listen to what people are saying externally and really challenge ourselves: Are we doing everything we can? I try to be

as progressive as possible. So we had all the firms come in and pitch their view on the world of ERM. I started going, wow, OK, there's something here.

I was really a bit worried that our directors would start saying, well, what are you doing on ERM? ... Quite frankly, we took a deep dive into all the areas that manage risk on behalf of the company, and we thought we were doing a pretty good job of managing risk. We went out and just really dug into the areas, like particularly finance and the treasury risk — that stuff is rock solid. We have always had very good discipline there. [We looked at] risk management as it relates to safety in our stores, risk management as it relates to other operational areas in the store, brand risk management. We said, OK, we do a lot of this and it's embedded in what we do, which we thought was really good.

And then we said, but do we have sort of common language across the enterprise, are we talking about the bigger risks? And the answer was, no, not really. So we needed common terminology, common standards around measuring risk, etc. We [concluded] it would be smart to create a governing body.

Even though the company tries to avoid bureaucracy and excessive formal meetings, it formed a governing body, called it the Risk Management Council, and populated it with the individuals actually performing the hands-on risk management. So instead of the CEO's direct reports, such as executive vice presidents, the Council was composed of lower ranking managers, such as vice presidents and senior vice presidents. The council has about 15 members and the CAE heads it up. There are other companies with similar risk councils, but the composition tends to be oriented toward CEO direct reports.

The company has a director of compliance who heads up the ERM process but is not a member of the internal audit team. Auditors, though, perform the in-depth, granular risk assessments by functional areas. The risk assessments are updated every six months, and the risks are rated red, yellow, or green, based on likelihood and magnitude. Once a quarter, the compliance director and internal audit directors generate an unranked list of the company's top 10 risks. The CAE explains:

We take each top 10 risk and identify all of the mitigation plans that are in place, and then we [include] the four different categories that would make the risk fall into a top 10 place.... The first is exposure greater than $100 million; the second one is significant negative impact to reputation; the third one is potential for criminal and/or government fines; and the fourth one is significant business and/or system change. We give this information to the board. It gives them a context of why we think it's a top 10 risk because we have other high-rated risks in the company that may not bubble up to a top 10 risk.

Each risk is also assigned to a level of preparedness — high, medium, and low — and reaction time — high (green, less than a quarter), medium (yellow, two to three quarters), and low (red, greater than three quarters). The risk council has to approve the list and the assessments, but this is usually just a formality. The auditors are experts in the functional areas and tend to be quite thorough.

Another large company, an international consumer products manufacturer, has a risk council headed by the CEO and populated by his direct reports. The evolution of the ERM process at this company is revealing. The CAE describes it:

> [ERM] started in corporate audit primarily because corporate audit is one of the few departments that has its tentacles all over the world ... and knows how to work and create processes. Corporate audit was deployed some 12 years ago or so to create a risk management process, and so it did.

The process was established along the lines of a traditional ERM program — brainstorming sessions, risk committees, heat maps, charts, key risk performance indicators, and risks localized by country. But as the process matured and stabilized, people inside the company began to complain that the process was a "waste of time," the risks didn't change, and the risks were being managed anyway. The company simplified the process accordingly and removed much of the excess formality. Simple forms replaced elaborate, detailed reports.

But the risk council was really the executive committee of the corporation. It was a large committee and ERM was usually deferred to the end of its regular meetings, where it was given short shrift as committee members rushed to catch plane flights.

In 2008, everything changed. With the global crisis, what had been a mere exercise became reality. Before that there had been the usual trappings of an ERM system — heat maps, elaborate charts, and risk discussions — but derived internally. Suddenly, prices for energy and grain exploded. The company endured, but there was a general feeling that the response was sluggish and outside expertise would have been very helpful.

The company concluded that it needed to get serious about ERM; to make the risk meetings "real meetings" and not "prepare-for-the-board meetings." It also moved ERM from the internal audit department to the controller's department, reporting to the CFO. This was done because of a belief that the internal audit department should *not* own the ERM process; that it should be a separate, independent entity and that the ERM process should be owned by an "operating" department. The controller is now the CRO.

We have two large successful companies with model ERM programs but whose ERM processes are drastically different. Another difference we observed was formal versus informal processes. One company has a disciplined approach to launching projects in foreign countries: Form small joint ventures, put key personnel "on the ground," test the waters, and then expand over time. Naturally, their ERM process is relatively formal. Another company values its "great conversational approach," says a board member. Not surprisingly, ERM is relatively informal there.

A key observation about processes that should permeate all organizations is this: All risk management should be incorporated into the ERM system. A risk management effort that is outside ERM creates a "risk silo" environment that is a throwback to the old pre-ERM days and should be avoided. Instead, ERM should give rise to a culture of risk management that cuts across all segments and levels of the organization.

Standard & Poor's is quite specific in the consideration of a *risk management culture* in its evaluation of a company's credit rating: "Since the third quarter of last year [2008], our analysts have begun to incorporate specific ERM discussions into their regular meetings with the companies we rate, focusing on risk management culture and strategic risk management as two universally applicable aspects of ERM."[43]

Along these lines, a report issued by the Senior Supervisors Group in connection with the global economic crisis reached these conclusions about the importance of sharing risk information across the organization:

> Firms that understood quickly the kinds and scale of risks they faced and that generally avoided significant losses through year-end 2007 relied on information from many parts of their businesses and communicated that information both up to senior management and across businesses.
>
> In contrast, the existence of organizational "silos" in the structures of some firms appeared to be detrimental to the firms' performance during the turmoil. Silos tended to compartmentalize information: in some cases, information gathered by one business line was not shared with other business lines where the information would have been useful. This inadvertent diversion or withholding of key information left different business areas to make decisions in isolation and in ignorance of other areas' insights.[44]

Boards need the risk assessments performed in an integrated way. Along these lines, organizations should develop a common approach, language, and method. A CAE comments:

> One of the things that a lot of companies are struggling with about ERM, and I encourage you to think about this, is where there are silos about managing risk. In our case, we have corporate compliance roll up to the general counsel. They had their own risk assessments going on; we [internal auditors] were doing ours. It was very confusing. They were very bureaucratic. They were putting together notebooks and they were making people go through this risk exercise that took something like four days. People were really disregarding them. And that's when they asked me to take it over. So we combined the two efforts and now we have one enterprise risk assessment.

It is important to know when to step up the process from opinions of risks to informed opinions. One company began a simple ERM process but eventually decided some measurement around some of the risks would improve decision-making. Recognizing the imprecision in the metrics did not prevent them from moving forward. This company began to develop macroeconomic models on certain risks, and was also able to take other subjective risks and convert them into some informal numbers so the real exposure could be understood and the risks could be properly ranked. For example, the company was able to take supply chain risk and convert it into understandable rankings using more financial data and subjective metrics. The CAE elaborates:

> It takes the [senior managers'] subjective risk perception and gives it some bookends and something that becomes explicit within the organization in terms of understanding: "Well, what is our risk profile, really?" and "What is our risk attitude, really?" And an example of that would be the factory risk assessments that we've been doing in 2010, where we've really gone in and tried

to pull from the experts what are their subjective risk assessments and then try to calibrate those and put those into a model that actually means something, and it can be used as a decision-making tool to allocate resources.

This same company has recognized the value of modeling the hard way. The ERM executive comments:

> We have a really good idea of what the variance in our earnings is going to be and how much risk is inherent in the process that we're engaged in right now. And when you think about what has happened — if you look at our sales — what has happened since the beginning of 2007 through present, even though it has been really, quite frankly, cataclysmic, it has become, believe it or not, pretty easy to forecast.... We're sort of in a, if I can use this term, stable catastrophe right now.

Another major lesson for this company was similar to an earlier point about using outside experts: The organization, a retailer, now routinely incorporates macroeconomic data into its ERM systems.

Best practices in the ERM process area can be summarized as follows:

- **Design the processes around the organization's culture to maximize buy-in from managers and the CEO, and to leverage the organization's existing resources.**
- **Establish a governing body for risk — a risk council, for example — and empower the group to monitor the management of risks. Clearly define its relationship with the board.**
- **Ensure that all risk management occurs in the ERM structure — no risk silos.**
- **Make clear the ownership of risks and the ERM process.**
- **Use, to the extent appropriate, the internal auditors' skills and expertise in the ERM process.**
- **Use good risk metrics when possible, even if their exact precision is in question. Use independent, objective data sources as needed.**
- **Encourage the evolution of the ERM system to fine-tune it or to meet changing conditions.**

For CAEs and audit professionals: **1) Thoroughly understand your organization's entire ERM process to be able to accurately provide feedback to those charged with risk oversight; and 2) conduct assessments of the adequacy and effectiveness of the organization's risk management processes.**

Chapter 11

RISK FRAMEWORK

A critical element in any well-designed ERM system is an underlying framework. ISO 31000 defines an ERM framework as follows:

Risk management framework

> ...set of components that provide the foundations and organizational arrangements for designing, implementing, monitoring (2.28), reviewing, and continually improving risk management (2.2) throughout the organization.
>
> NOTE 1: The foundations include the policy, objectives, mandate, and commitment to manage risk (2.1).
>
> NOTE 2: The organizational arrangements include plans, relationships, accountabilities, resources, processes, and activities.
>
> NOTE 3: The risk management framework is embedded within the organization's overall strategic and operational policies and practices. [ISO Guide 73:2009, definition 2.1.1][45]

The framework is integral to the ERM effort, but it can provide only a structure. The actual operation of the system radiates from the framework. While there is some general agreement about the characteristics that a strong framework should have, there are differences of opinion as to how a framework should approach the operation of the system itself.

There are several ERM frameworks available to organizations as they implement ERM, all of which were promulgated by respected groups from around the world. There are many similarities among the frameworks but also significant differences:

- *Enterprise Risk Management – Integrated Framework: Executive Summary*, issued by COSO in the United States (2004).

- *Internal Control: Revised Guidance for Directors on the Combined Code*, issued by the Financial Reporting Council (Turnbull Review Group), United Kingdom (2005).

- *The Australian and New Zealand Standard on Risk Management (AS/NZ 4360)*, issued by Standards Australia and Standards New Zealand Technical Committee (2004).

- *ISO 31000, Risk management — Principles and guidelines*, issued by the International Organization for Standardization (ISO, 2009).

The COSO framework is built around a three-dimensional representation of ERM, depicted in Figure 3 as a cube. On the top of the cube is the objectives dimension — strategic, operations, reporting, and compliance. The front of the cube contains the processes dimension — internal environment, objective setting, event identification, risk assessment, risk response, control activities, information & communication, and monitoring. Finally, the side of the cube depicts the organizational dimension — subsidiary, business unit, division, and entity level.

Figure 3: The COSO ERM Cube

COSO explains the rationale behind the cubic approach: "There is a direct relationship between objectives, which are what an entity strives to achieve, and enterprise risk management components, which represent what is needed to achieve them.... This depiction portrays the ability to focus on the entirety of an entity's enterprise risk management, or by objectives category, component, entity unit, or any subset thereof."[46]

The COSO document was the first of the modern efforts at establishing an ERM framework, and it was generally accepted by U.S. companies. But, over time, the COSO framework failed to evolve, and organizations realized that it would be difficult to build an ERM structure around it, verbatim. Several of the organizations in our study revealed that they were using a variation of the COSO framework to anchor ERM. A major U.S. retailer with worldwide operations combines the COSO framework with ISO 31000 to meet its needs. A major technology company uses a "derivative" of the COSO approach but retains the COSO "anchor."

One large consumer products company has its own version of COSO. The company's CAE explains it this way:

> At our company, we have what we call our global control standard, and it's based on COSO. [But] COSO is more operating and financial risk versus the other types of risks [we encounter]. And so in our risk management process, we're talking about things that could dramatically

impact the company. I think all of these things tie into the COSO framework, but I would say our overall ERM is more "COSO on steroids," where we use COSO for routine and non-routine risks in every entity around the world.

That keys into our risk committees, which are local risk committees. Then the divisional risk committees [feed] to the corporate risk committees. So the most important things bubble up to the top.

[As to COSO], it's not a check the box. I would say it's "companytized" — we started with COSO and said, how do you operationalize this? We created our own brand which we called the global control standard and then [shaped it] around the attributes and the policies of how all these things need to work inside of the company.

Although it was widely adopted in one form or another, the COSO framework was not without its critics. Some believed it focused too heavily on internal issues rather than the impact of external forces — internal context versus internal *and* external contexts. Others believed it was too complicated and lengthy, which made it difficult to implement. ISO 31000 actually distills many of the strong points of COSO and AS/NZ 4360, and in its brief existence, has earned accolades from ERM participants worldwide.

ISO 31000 is designed to be "principles-based" as opposed to prescriptive. In fact, the document itself uses the term "generic" to describe its approach. The idea is that an organization will adopt the very broad principles of sound ERM as identified in ISO 31000 and then adapt the framework to its own particular set of circumstances. In this way, it exists as a valuable tool to furnish structure and effectiveness for the ERM effort.

ISO 31000 provides this explanation of its ultimate goal:

> Although the practice of risk management has been developed over time and within many sectors in order to meet diverse needs, the adoption of consistent processes within a comprehensive framework can help to ensure that risk is managed effectively, efficiently, and coherently across an organization. The generic approach described in this International Standard provides the principles and guidelines for managing any form of risk in a systematic, transparent, and credible manner and within any scope and context.[47]

There is an implication in the standard that organizations will integrate ERM into strategy and all decision processes. It will be a routine component of the array of tools management has at its disposal to perform its job effectively. Organizations may want to consult ISO 31000's Figure 1 (p. vii in ISO 31000), which is helpful in its depiction of the relationship between the ERM principles, the framework for managing risk, and the risk management processes.

An effective ERM program must have a solid foundation in its chosen, tailored framework. As in building construction, a strong foundation will provide the support needed to maintain the integrity of the structure. The same issue applies here. A weak framework will undermine the ERM effort and render it much less effective.

A best practice, then, is: **Develop the ERM program around a strong framework initially, be it COSO, ISO 31000, a combination of the two, or some other valid framework. But adapt the framework to the needs of the organization and then continually monitor its effectiveness. Adjust it to changing conditions as needed.**

For CAEs and audit professionals: **1) Benchmark your organization's ERM process against a widely accepted ERM framework; and 2) assist management in communicating the importance of ERM to the organization.**

Chapter 12

BOARD AND C-SUITE RELATIONSHIP

One key to a strong ERM system is effective interaction between the board and the CEO, representing the C-suite. Because the CEO implements and operates the ERM system, the board members must trust him or her to share relevant information with them and keep them fully informed of the major risks facing the organization. It is impossible for a board to fulfill its risk oversight responsibilities if the CEO keeps it in the dark, or glosses over the existence of major risks or the organization's level of control over them. Although a strong ERM leader can make a difference here, as can having the ERM process reviewed by internal audit, the relationship between the board and CEO is vital.

Additionally, the CEO can set the tone at the top and the risk culture of the organization. Boards must know and understand the risk culture in their organizations. Many stories have come up since the financial crisis that suggested the risk culture and tone at the top (toward risk) were severely lacking in some organizations that experienced financial collapse.

Why do many organizations seem to miss major risks and fail to properly assess and manage them? Weak risk oversight by the board is typically a culprit. Often, the root problem is that the board was not fully informed of risks, rendering it toothless. An ERM process implemented by management with risk oversight by the board cannot exhibit the twists and turns of a parkour[48] approach. It must be well focused with strong planning and execution, and ultimately that focus depends on the CEO.

In one company, after a discussion between the CEO, a risk consultant, and board member, the board member acknowledged he had never heard the CEO talk about those specific risks before. Boards must insist that CEOs avoid keeping key risk information to themselves. Building and fostering the CEO-board relationship means creating an open, continuous, and two-way dialog between the board and the CEO.

Building and fostering that relationship also means ensuring the board is continually receiving high-quality risk information. This topic touched a nerve with several executives and directors, as the following comments illustrate. One director acknowledged the problem this way: "CEOs can share only what they want to share." Similarly, an executive expressed his concerns: "The question for most board members [is this]: Are they getting good information? And I would argue that, in some cases, they are not." Another director added:

> Your oversight is only as good as the data you are getting. There is no real independent way to get it. You can make sure you know the people, try to meet a lot of them, the key ones, particularly, and others, get a feel for what is going on and watch their body language, how they act around their superiors, what the mood is. But if you have a dishonest guy in charge, you have to get rid of him. That is where all these companies have gotten in trouble. Where they said, "You know, …we've got to go along with Joe."

As one director emphasized, good CEOs are critical: "In business, the most important thing is the people and the most important person is the person in charge, the CEO. The most important thing is that you have confidence [in the CEO], you have to ask questions … because that is going to set the standard." The importance of the board staying ahead of the risk curve cannot be overemphasized because it is critical. As another director pointed out, "If a company stalls for more than a month, it's very hard to redeem growth trajectory. Boards really are accountable for the health of the enterprise to the shareholders."

One director explained his new expectations: "They've got to give you everything you want, and I mean everything." But there is a balance that must be achieved in reporting to the board — not too much and not too little. One board requires the detail be put in an appendix so that, as one director quips, "guys like me can go wander back there forever." Under the CEO's direction, the CFO at this company gives the board an advance deck of risk information and walks the board through most of the detail and knows the numbers so thoroughly that he can respond appropriately when there's a question. "Let me call up right here. It's in your appendix, but let me get it for you right here. He knows every single page … a lot of guys can't do that."

One director commented, "When you have a good CEO who is open and transparent, you are able to get good [risk] information. When you don't, it's the board's responsibility to create an environment where they get the information they need … and not be passive or be managed." One of the key motivators for CEOs to get up to speed on ERM is when boards ask more risk questions. One board member noted, "I think one of the ways that CEOs become influenced is for their boards to ask for it [risk information]." Of course, the director's meetings are quite packed and can be hectic, but one director emphasized the importance of prioritizing risk discussions: "If we have something serious to talk about, we don't let the agenda get in the way. There is usually some dialog that is helpful for the CEO and board to get over and that's very good. That practice really helped us."

One director explains that once their CEO discusses the specifics of how he intends to reach target earnings per share, such as geographic segment contributions and target margins, the board holds him accountable for subsequent performance against these targets, not against prior period results. In this way, the board can gauge how well the CEO understands the business. And this is a buildup of trust in the CEO.

Once that trust is there, it enables learning together: "If you came back and said, we missed it [the EPS target], the Japanese cut the price at Thanksgiving, I buy that. That's OK. And if it happens two years in a row, we ought to think about cutting the price. There are acceptable reasons for missing … but as a board we have to understand that."

According to another director, the key is for the CEO and board to work together:

> We sort of learned together, and as a result I think the process for us was a discovery process … but we were thinking strategically, probably because my role was a very strategic one here. So that was unique … that he [the CEO] and I had the luxury of collaborating for a decade around strategy and risk. I simply nudge him now and then. It was a methodology and a strategic approach to risk management, which led us to sort of an enterprise risk management platform, risk committee, risk map, and all of those things.

However, even good CEOs are human and make mistakes. When asked why CEOs neglect major risks, one director stated, "They think they're right. Of course they think they're right. They are not trying to do something that they think is wrong. But just because you're right now, you might not be right in 18 months." Not being "right" with respect to enterprise-level risks results in lost opportunities, lost value, and excessive costs. Best practice boards take their risk oversight responsibility seriously and do not get a false sense of security simply because they've been told the company is practicing ERM. One executive revealed the danger: "Risk management, it's very easy to form a base exercise and just check the box, OK we had the meeting, we talked about these things, done. You know? Let's put it away 'til next quarter or next meeting. Who cares? It's one of the very easy things to fake."

One of the difficulties in building and fostering the CEO-board relationship is a result of the conflicting risks facing the CEO, who likely wants to keep his or her position and reputation, and the board, which is trying to manage both the short-term and long-term value of the organization. The salvage yard of corporations is littered with executives who managed their own personal risks but left the company bearing the larger and more permanent risks. This risk divergence can inevitably lead to tension between the board and the CEO.

Sometimes the only solution to the trust issue is to replace the CEO. One director said, "I think the most important thing that the board has an obligation to the shareholders to do is to hire and fire the CEO. No board in America, I bet you 10 to one, would ever say, 'Wow, we fired the CEO too soon.' They never say that. Never." Another director added, "We had a guy who wouldn't give us very good information, so I turned to my board members [in an executive session] and said, 'This is BS.' He [the CEO] prided himself in trying to keep his board in the dark. My assistant calls me Doctor Death. I will tell you we ended up firing this guy because he did not know how to work with his board."

But it is not just the CEO who is important to risk management and oversight — other executives can be equally important. One company upgraded its strategy people to help manage the link between risk and strategy. The director noted, "There's got to be a very, very tight linkage between the strategic planning process and the risk management process. The strategic planning process was extremely weak [when starting ERM] and it is very, very robust now." Another company's changing business model led to new risks and a need for new talent to manage that risk. "We've got management that can't move inventory correctly. You look at talent in R&D, in manufacturing ... totally different skill sets. So we've changed out the entire management. We've [now] got a road here we like and we've got a CEO we like."

Furthermore, better boards seek outside help when appropriate. One director explained the importance of getting an outside perspective:

> The risks to the company are what you're there to protect against and you're supposed to see around the corner and anticipate; and most of the risks are strategic business risks. There is [also] the outlier risk that somebody does some impropriety.
>
> But that's not the risk that kills most companies. The risk that kills most companies and why they only last 20 years, 40 percent, and why 60 percent are gone after 40 years is business risk. You need to understand your market and your competitive dynamics and you didn't have the

right talent. There's only a few things that go wrong, right? You were asleep and the market changed. You didn't have the right people. You weren't challenging the people to anticipate around the corner. You weren't bringing in objective info that was contrary to managements' viewpoints so that you had a check and balance on how they see the world. It's very simple. It's just hard to do.

It is important to recall that the goal of ERM is to "create, protect, and enhance shareholder value."[49] As such, CEOs should understand that directors are not there to tie their hands or micromanage every issue. An ERM process and proper risk oversight should enable the organization and the CEO to meet their objectives and achieve the value targets. But the key to doing that is to take the right risks and know the risks that are being taken. CEOs may not always appreciate board criticism, but good board risk oversight will help them meet their goals.

Best practice in the CEO-board relationship can be summarized as follows: **To build trust and engage in vigorous risk dialog, boards must hold the CEO accountable for providing them with high-quality risk information. The information should provide transparency and be sufficient for the board to exercise its oversight responsibilities effectively.**

Chapter 13

THE BOARD AS A RISK

In addition to the CEO-board relationship, several directors pointed out that a common risk not addressed by the ERM process is the board itself. Given the board's pivotal role in overseeing the link between ERM and strategy and in working with the CEO, this risk is not trivial. Of course, no ERM team lists the board on the risk heat map or the risk dashboard; if they did, it could be one of the top risks. Consider one director's bold statement when asked if CEOs understand risk: "Yes, I think most do, and the ones that don't are the ones the boards need to hack off. And remember, the length of a company's life is 20 years for 40 percent of corporations. Forty percent! Almost half are gone in 20 years. So where are you in your lifeline as a company? Are you in your first five years? Are you in the last five years?"

One obvious and somewhat historic risk related to the board is the structure of the board and, specifically, its independence. Having independent directors and the percentage of independent directors is considered by many to be major issues concerning the board's ability to implement proper oversight. A number of corporate governance groups monitor items such as board independence as well as issues such as whether the CEO is also the chairman. From a risk oversight perspective, it is better to have more board independence and oversight.

One very experienced board member seemed especially concerned about board independence and suggested that several major U.S. company failures correlated with a lack of board independence: "In my humble opinion, the independence of the board was one of the major issues. I mean, if you don't have independent board members, nothing is going to work." As previously noted, the Dodd-Frank Act mandates risk committees and gives the Board of Governors of the Federal Reserve System the power to determine the number of directors that is considered appropriate. Given the elevation of risk oversight, boards may want to reconsider the makeup of the board and the number of independent directors.

As previously noted, the SEC now requires registrants to discuss "whether and why" the principal executive officer and board chairman are the same.[50] The very fact that the SEC is requiring companies to disclose this relationship and the board's role in risk oversight highlights the importance of the issue. The SEC also suggested (but did not mandate) that companies consider disclosing the reporting lines for those who oversee risk management. The SEC is probably concerned that CROs who report directly to other C-level officers and do not have dotted line reporting to a board-level committee may not be as effective in their jobs.

Presumably, the SEC would like to avoid the situation where C-level officers prevent enterprise risk information from being considered by the board. Recent federal sentencing guidelines support this structure by stating that an effective compliance and ethics program should have the head of that program reporting directly to the governing authority (i.e., to the board).[51] How can boards provide independent risk oversight if they do not separate the CEO and chairman or their reporting lines are blurred? One director noted that it was important for all boards to meet in sessions that did not include management to determine "anything that's bugging anybody."

In addition to these board structure-related risks, directors identified several other board-related risks. Directors felt strongly about having peers (other board members) getting involved and being proactive about governance and oversight. "Getting a bunch of very passive board members who aren't engaged — that's a risk," added one director. Another director noted that new directors can make a big impact on areas such as risk oversight.

The ERM process in one company was moving slowly until two key board changes occurred. The first was a change in the mix of board members — as more and more independent members joined the board, ERM seemed more likely to progress. The second board change was the arrival of a new board member who had seen ERM implemented in another company and felt strongly about ERM becoming operational. The ERM leader describes it: "One of our [new] directors is into ERM in a monumental way. Really, really into it and so, quite frankly, put pressure on other board members and would continually push for more information, more transparency with respect to how the company's managing its risks. Were it not for this effort, I'm wondering … whether or not we [the ERM team] really would have ever gotten in front of the audit committee, quite frankly."

It is not only getting the right risk information to the board that is critical. Board members must work closely together and trust each other. A director elaborates: "I know in each of these companies that the people on the committee that I am not on are doing their job and they are doing it as well as anybody." One board member explained that it is also critical to have a board that does not play games — that is willing to be open and transparent: "I would say, without exception, that everybody on the board … recognizes the importance of this. So not only was I pounding and pushing, pushing hard [for ERM], there was a constant nudge coming from everybody else." Another director added, "Having a regard and confidence in your board members' ability and attitude and approach is more than critical."

One caveat in this area is for the board to not oversee risk management in silos. As noted previously, some organizations map out risk responsibilities to ensure all risks are covered by a board-level committee. Because ERM is really *enterprise-wide* risk management and makes an attempt to avoid silo management of risks, boards must be careful not to make the same mistake. Communications between committees and full board oversight of risks is essential to integrated risk oversight.

According to several directors, boards must learn when it is time to get risk help from external advisors. Sometimes this is obvious because the risks are so large that risk specialists are essential to keeping the organization running. At other times, the risks are related to changes in the business, and risk advisors can be sought out to help the transition.

One director felt very strongly about risk oversight and brought in an external risk advisor to train the board and top executives on ERM best practices and to learn what other companies' ERM practices and processes looked like. After that initial session, the entire management team began to take risk seriously. As that company expanded into new markets and took on new risks, additional advisors were brought in to help the company understand the risks and predicted trends in the new markets. Of course, it must be emphasized that in spite of all the effort taken by management and the board, some boards can only do a high-level oversight of risks, so a sound relationship between the CEO and the board is essential.

A best practice to limit the risk of the board itself can be summarized as: **Boards are independent of management in their risk oversight activities and provide for direct interaction with CROs. Board members themselves are trained on risk management, are enthusiastic about the process, and ensure that their oversight efforts are integrated and include outside experts when needed.**

CAE's and audit professionals: **1) Perform a review of the organization's overall governance process, including risk management processes and reporting, and report accordingly; 2) ensure that there are appropriate and ongoing communication- and information-sharing processes with the organization's CRO; and 3) assist the organization's risk and control units to identify opportunities to leverage common processes or technologies across the risk and control units.**

Chapter 14

INTERNAL AUDITING

Risk oversight is a new practice in many organizations, and boards need some sort of assurance that it is working. One CAE explained a concern that the board would begin quizzing her department about the organization's ERM efforts, which motivated her to do a "deep dive" into all risk management activities. She was surprised at the outcome. The risk management efforts were not as strong as she supposed. Boards may want to consider a similar deep examination of the risk practices at their organizations.

The review can initially be kept simple. Every quarter, one company asks all board members to evaluate the effectiveness of the ERM process on a 1 (not effective) to 5 (highly effective) scale. Both the CFO and CRO receive the results. Of course, the goal is a 5. Another company just asks the audit committee members what they want. An executive explains:

> Each year I actually do a survey of all our audit committee members, just asking: Are we presenting the *right topics* to them? Did they like the way the *agenda* was set? Did they like the *materials*? Did they like the *format*? Just for me to get feedback because I set the agenda and make sure the materials are produced. So as a part of that, I ask them what they'd like to see *more* of, *less* of.

Of course, given the stakes with mismanaging risks and the potential lost value, boards should go beyond a simple approach and take a more serious examination of risk processes. Assurance on the risk management process helps the board understand the organization, the executives, and the strategy more comprehensively. Because ERM can add considerable value to an organization, that assurance also helps the board know it is on the right trajectory to creating that value.

Boards can gain some assurance on ERM and risk oversight in a number of ways, including:

- Benchmarking their ERM process against other companies.
- Using ERM maturity models that assess several attributes of an ERM system on how "mature" the attributes are.
- Being well-informed about ERM.
- Evaluating the C-level's approach to ERM.
- Hiring external consultants to review their ERM process.
- Employing the ERM assessment tool in Appendix B.
- Using the internal audit staff.

With regard to using internal audit, we found that CAEs and their staffs exhibited a variety of roles in ERM and risk oversight. However, one informal trend surfaced. Although many companies initially had

Improving Board Risk Oversight Through Best Practices

ERM reporting to the CAE, some moved ERM reporting to the CFO. But even those companies still include the internal audit department in their ERM efforts.

The IIA has taken a clear position on the role of the CAE in risk management: "Internal auditing is an independent, objective assurance and consulting activity. Its core role with regard to ERM is to provide objective assurance to the board on the effectiveness of risk management."[52] Figure 4 shows core roles internal auditors can do, can do with safeguards, and cannot do with respect to risk management.[53]

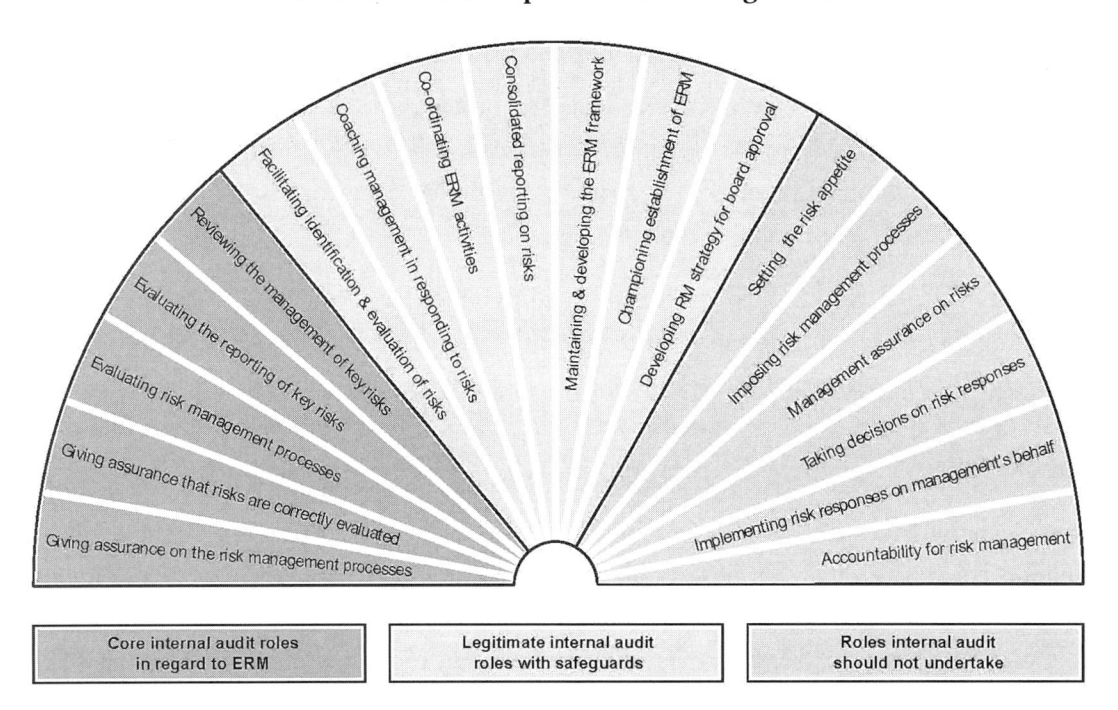

Figure 4: Roles the Internal Auditor Can Do, Can Do with Safeguards, and Cannot Do with Respect to Risk Management

Core internal audit roles in regard to ERM:
- Giving assurance on the risk management processes
- Giving assurance that risks are correctly evaluated
- Evaluating risk management processes
- Evaluating the reporting of key risks
- Reviewing the management of key risks

Legitimate internal audit roles with safeguards:
- Facilitating identification & evaluation of risks
- Coaching management in responding to risks
- Co-ordinating ERM activities
- Consolidated reporting on risks
- Maintaining & developing the ERM framework
- Championing establishment of ERM
- Developing RM strategy for board approval

Roles internal audit should not undertake:
- Setting the risk appetite
- Imposing risk management processes
- Management assurance on risks
- Taking decisions on risk responses
- Implementing risk responses on management's behalf
- Accountability for risk management

(Source: The IIA, *The Role of Internal Auditing in Enterprise-wide Risk Management*, Position Statement, p. 3)

Appendix C highlights the various roles that internal audit can play in both ERM and in helping boards achieve their risk oversight objectives. One item included in Appendix C is assessing the ERM process. Obviously, internal auditors have the skills to review the ERM process and evaluate whether it is effective. Boards may want to consider having an audit of their risk processes. One very large global company in this study explained that its first ever audit of ERM would be done in 2011. Some typical evidence and procedures that internal auditors might do to assess the ERM process include:

- Reviewing current developments and trends to determine potential risks, and then reviewing any related controls.

- Reviewing corporate policies and board minutes to determine risk appetite, philosophy, etc.

- Reviewing risk evaluation reports.

Chapter 14: Internal Auditing

- Conducting interviews with management to determine risk, mitigation plans, and monitoring activities.
- Reviewing the adequacy and timeliness of risk reporting.
- Reviewing the appropriateness of reporting lines for risk reporting.
- Reviewing the completeness of management's risk analysis.[54]

Appendix C also includes some more specific value-added activities that auditors could do, including training boards, attending risk meetings, presenting at risk meetings, verifying the velocity of risks, etc. In addition to these practices, internal audit can be of value in numerous other ways.

One way that internal auditors can be involved is that they might be asked to *take the lead* on the initial ERM and risk oversight efforts. This occurred in several of the companies we interviewed. Clearly, CAEs are thought of very highly if they are given this role. Whether done by internal auditors or others, a more formal ERM process may be necessary to have proper board risk oversight. A few participants in this study noted that their companies had made the shift to a formal enterprise risk process. Later, the auditor's role may change and he or she may move into more of a risk consulting role.

Auditors also should *adapt audit plans* based on the information they learn from the risk efforts. One director explained: "[The CAE] is not part of the strategy planning process, but he and I sit down shortly thereafter and we go through the list of major risks that are in this book that we've got and I say, 'OK, what can we audit out of this? What's auditable?' And that gets built into the next year's audit plan."

In other cases, CAEs *own the governance process around risks*. One CAE noted:

> I'm actually speaking to our board in November about our ERM. I speak to them once a year. I lead the group and I am responsible for bubbling up the top risk, but I do not view myself as owning risk management. I view my role as owning the governance around risk management and ensuring that we are identifying the risks, and that the risks are being addressed, they're being mitigated, and that we're putting funding against the risks that we think are priority.

At other companies, *CAEs simply get involved when possible*. For example, at one company, "internal audit actually performs the granular risk assessments that provide the ability for us to bubble up what the top 10 risks are." Similarly, in another company, in spite of having a separate ERM function, the CAE assists the process by doing in-depth risk assessments by functional area. This assessment is updated every six months. From that, all risks are rated on likelihood and magnitude and sorted into red, yellow, or green. The CAE and the ERM team look at all the red risks and bubble them into the major (top 10) type risks. The process for filtering the top risks considers four categories — financial impact, negative impact to reputation, potential criminal or government fines, and significant business or system change.

At another company, the internal auditors *participate in both the emerging risk and strategic risk sessions*. The CAE explained:

> Once a year we also do a very deep dive and we actually just started this. This is new this year. A very deep dive into, separately, into our strategic risk. OK, so, the top 10 risk and the emerging

risk could include and do include strategic risk, but we do a separate analysis around strategic risk as connected to our strategic planning process. So I sit in on all of our strategic planning processes, all of the discussion around that, so people actually come and they pitch what they're going to do in terms of strategic initiative in the upcoming year. And I sit through all those presentations, as does the CEO and all his direct reports.

One CAE noted that once an ERM process is in place, the key challenge and role of internal audit was to *push the conversation* to the point that ERM becomes "a serious part of the conversation with senior leaders and the board." Pushing the conversation must be done carefully with the view of running the company better. One CAE explained: "We're still trying to find the right balance of how do we take the information and present it in such a way (to senior leaders and the board) to help run the company. Not just a reporting thing or a scare tactic." Another CAE expanded on the importance of the conversation about risk becoming a conversation about running the business better:

> You are a senior manager and all senior managers view that their job is to not only grow the company but to guard against the risk. If you walk in here and the only thing you talk about are the risks… what you are saying is that you are not doing your job. That is one of the reasons that we developed this conversation that I have with senior leaders. When I come in to talk about risk… I may even start the conversation by saying, "For us to get to that opportunity, what has to go right?"

Internal auditors can also play valuable roles in *reviewing the risk mitigation plans and level of preparedness*. A CAE explained their contribution:

> We define level of preparedness as how quickly would we be able to respond if, in fact, the risk became an issue to the company. And then we also look at it in terms of what level or degree of confidence do we have in the controls and the existing processes that protect us against that risk and what sort of confidence level do we have that what we do today would mitigate the risk if it really manifested itself into a big issue.
>
> And then we also look at it in terms of "high" — we say the reaction time for us to be able to react to the risk would be less than a quarter. Medium would be a reaction time of greater than two quarters. And low would be greater than three quarters it would take us to react to the risk. So that's a level of preparedness, and we assign that to each one of the top 10 risks.

At other companies, the *role of the CAE changed as the process changed*. One CAE explained that when ERM was initially adopted, internal audit played a big role in risk identification. Now that ERM is more sophisticated, the role of internal audit has been expanded. He explains:

> We're doing a lot more in planning, tracking, ensuring that those risks are mitigated to the extent that we can.
>
> That is the biggest thing (changes by internal audit). We are actually reviewing mitigation plans, ensuring funding is in place, ensuring people are taking action. We actually go back…

Chapter 14: Internal Auditing

> we use the audit team and others to go back and do the work to ensure that mitigation is being worked on and is complete. I think we've done a lot more to ensure that we are taking the actions that are needed to address those risks.

This review of the risk mitigation plans can be tied to the internal audit plan. One CAE called this risk mitigation process and the related ties to internal audit plans "*the biggest hammer.*" He explains:

> We do see it having an impact. We see the individual risk teams are open for suggestions, and probably the biggest hammer we have is that as we begin to get this information, I use it to inform my risk assessment. We will actually go in and take a look at these areas and see if they are doing anything about them. From the internal audit side, if we see areas that are not being addressed that potentially should be addressed, we can actually write up issues that have to be addressed.

Internal audit has connections in most aspects of the business and also has close relationships with many business leaders and risk owners. As such, internal audit can also play a key role in *developing the relationship between risks and strategy* for those particular business units. One CAE explains:

> We are finding our way into the strategy and business planning session. We track risks through to make sure they get into the business plan — that they are legitimately in the business plan. I think that was a big push. We are trying to extend the program into the everyday operation of the company.

This knowledge of the business processes combined with knowledge of ERM also enables internal audit to *improve the discussion and reporting of risks*. One CAE noted how they coordinate with risk managers and business owners to ensure that those owners understand the risk framework, risk common language, and the risk definitions. By sharing and communicating this information, the entire risk reporting system is more consistent, and it helps the company "link information from the bottom to the top."

One additional key role noted by one CAE was for the CAE *to build a relationship with the board members* to help them get the comfort they need. The CAE explained his understanding about the board's concern being "overall governance." He added, however, that the board is concerned about the CAE view of the ERM process. He explains:

> When I talk to the board or the audit committee... their (the board's) questions are around whether I am talking to the right people, whether I am getting support. Is the company open and those types of things? They have to believe that I am getting the right kind of information. Are the actions of management or their comments to commitment really being followed through? What is it that I am not seeing? We have a lot of conversations about those types of things.

Of course, for the internal auditors to add value, boards must determine how good the auditors are in the risk area. One CAE explained why the auditors in their company are seen differently and used in the ERM process:

We are not a traditional audit shop here; we do a lot of business process improvement, and we're much more tied to a lot of our strategic initiatives. And so, while compliance is important, and we do compliance, it represents only about 30 percent of what we do in our total time. The other 70 percent is really risk mitigation, working on initiatives to improve business processes, working to identify where there are opportunities in the company to connect the dots better with each other.

Best practice in ERM assurance can be stated this way: **Boards regularly evaluate the effectiveness of risk management and risk oversight processes, principally through the resources of the internal audit department and/or outside advisors with the use of appropriate tools.**

For CAE's and audit professionals: **1) Assess tone or the risk culture across the organization and report accordingly; and 2) be prepared to objectively discuss the organization's tone and risk culture in executive sessions with the audit committee.**

Conclusion

As ERM has grown in popularity and importance, organizations are placing more emphasis on enhancing the effectiveness of risk management in their own operations. This motivation — and some regulatory prodding — has been somewhat successful in strengthening the link between an organization's ERM system and its board and stimulating the board to become more engaged in the ERM system through its oversight responsibilities.

But there is anecdotal evidence that the involvement of some boards in ERM may be a "formality" or even "window dressing" that actually has little impact on the effectiveness of their ERM systems. Some believe that a fundamental misunderstanding of ERM and its potential may be the source of much of this.

It was our goal with this study to learn how organizations have effectively engaged their boards in their ERM systems and to develop a series of "best practices" that would be available for other organizations to use in strengthening their own risk management mechanisms.

We found that many of these best practices require more effort than they do money in their implementation, and it is not necessary to build elaborate and costly infrastructures to engage boards in the ERM system. Rather, the single most important variable in the board-ERM equation is management and board commitment to the system. Without that, no quantity of best practices will be truly effective. And that commitment can be obtained "free of charge."

Leveraging an organization's strengths is another key component in the equation. Good internal audit departments have the requisite skills and organizational knowledge to be leaders in the effort. In virtually all of our best practices companies, the CAE was a major player in board oversight of ERM and made important contributions to the understanding and structure of the board-ERM link.

Weak board oversight of risk has long been a glaring problem in modern society. From exploding credit default swaps, to the catastrophic Gulf of Mexico oil spill, to the deadly radiation spewing from damaged nuclear reactors in Japan, to even the five-foot rip in the fuselage of a jet airliner at 34,000 feet, monumental risks abound, many virtually unanticipated. It is clear that board oversight of risk must be improved and it must happen quickly. Well-managed organizations are taking this necessity to heart and are finding benefits of a magnitude not even the most optimistic of them expected.

Appendix A

SUMMARY OF BEST PRACTICES

1. Management should present to the board annually a deep dive on the ERM process and on the significant risks facing the organization and should provide updates of the significant risks and the related action plans at the quarterly board meetings.

2. To assess and have confidence in the risk information provided by management, directors must have a thorough understanding of the business and industry.

3. Compose the board's membership so that it has the diversity of skills and experiences necessary to fulfill its risk oversight responsibilities. Boards should continually assess their own talents and skills related to risk management and risk oversight.

4. A board should have a process to assure that all the risks identified are appropriately assigned to the various committees for oversight responsibility. The audit committee can serve as the lead committee that assigns risks for oversight to various board committees or to the full board, which should retain oversight for strategic risks.

5. Assign to the entire board the responsibility for risk oversight of strategic risks as part of its strategy-planning deliberations.

6. Include in a heat map provided to the board an assessment of the velocity of each risk, and consider providing a report listing for each of the significant risks impact, likelihood, and velocity.

7. The board and individual directors should assess their ERM knowledge and determine what training and education are needed to be able to perform risk oversight responsibilities.

8. Scan the environment often and critically, prioritize the recalibration of the top tier risk set, and have a mechanism in place to evaluate and incorporate important emerging risks into the system.

9. The reporting system should be tailored to the needs of the organization.

10. Reporting is sufficiently detailed to allow the board members to recognize and understand the key risks facing the organization and interconnectedness. Identifying five to 20 key risks seems optimal; some organizations elect to report on more.

11. Reporting is routine and occurs frequently.

12. Reporting includes updates on the status of management action plans related to key risks.

13. Although primary reporting should be to the designated committees or individual directors, every director receives informative risk reports.

14. Directors are trained to understand the organization's key risks and the management of them. For some directors, this will necessitate training in ERM generally.

15. Risk oversight is independent of the organization's CEO, but the CEO is part of the risk-management dialog. Risk reporting is direct to the board members without filtering, scrubbing, or diluting.

16. The entire reporting process is iterative. Information flows both ways — to the board and from the board in the form of feedback on the actual risk management and the quality of the reporting itself.

17. Design the processes around the organization's culture to maximize buy-in from managers and the CEO and to leverage the organization's existing resources.

18. Establish a governing body for risk — a risk council, for example — and empower the group to monitor the management of risks. Clearly define its relationship with the board.

19. Ensure that all risk management occurs in the ERM structure — no risk silos.

20. Make clear the ownership of risks and the ERM process.

21. Use, to the extent appropriate, the internal auditors' skills and expertise in the ERM process.

22. Use good risk metrics when possible, even if their exact precision is in question. Use independent, objective data sources as needed.

23. Encourage the evolution of the ERM system to fine-tune it or to meet changing conditions.

24. Develop the ERM program around a strong framework initially, be it COSO, ISO 31000, a combination of the two, or some other valid framework. But adapt the framework to the needs of the organization and then continually monitor its effectiveness. Adjust it to changing conditions as needed.

25. To build trust and engage in vigorous risk dialog, boards must hold the CEO accountable for providing them with high-quality risk information. The information should provide transparency and be sufficient for the board to exercise its oversight responsibilities effectively.

26. Boards are independent of management in their risk oversight activities and provide for direct interaction with CROs. Board members themselves are trained on risk management, are enthusiastic about the process, and ensure that their oversight efforts are integrated and include outside experts when needed.

27. Boards regularly evaluate the effectiveness of risk management and risk oversight processes, principally through the resources of the internal audit department and/or outside advisors with the use of appropriate tools.

Appendix B

BOARD ASSESSMENT OF RISK OVERSIGHT AND ERM: A TOOL

In recent work, the authors found that the number one tool used by organizations to manage risk is not some sophisticated modeling tool or even a risk assessment exercise: It is having a conversation about risks with management and with and among the board. The tool presented here is not meant to *replace* that conversation but should be used to *ignite* it.

For each question for which the board believes there is a lack of consensus, the board should have a discussion about why it is not following this practice. In some cases, the questions are rooted in mandated regulations. In other cases, they are considered a best practice by many organizations and by the research team.

1. The board and the organization have a rigorous strategic plan that incorporates all major and emerging risks.
2. The board is comfortable that management has identified all enterprise-level risks.
3. The board has a clearly defined risk oversight process and has clearly established risk responsibility.
4. The organization has a CRO or ERM leader with direct line reporting to the board or a respective board committee.
5. Quarterly, the board reviews risk maps, risk dashboards, or related risk reporting.
6. The board and organization go beyond risk maps and generate risk action plans as well as related risk metrics.
7. Corporate decision-making includes a discussion of the potential risks embedded in those decisions.
8. The organization is prepared for a Standard & Poor's or Moody's assessment of its ERM process.
9. The board is informed of emerging risks timely.
10. The board has received ERM training.
11. Executives openly share all risk information with board committees.
12. The organization has had no major risk debacles in the past fiscal period.
13. Executives and management-level risk committees have adequate resources and training to identify and manage risks.
14. Important risk information is streamlined and reported to the appropriate executives and board-level committees promptly.

15. ERM is viewed as a critical way to create value and grow the organization, while taking the appropriate risks.
16. The organization identifies the risks related to compensation plans.
17. Performance is evaluated in relation to the risks taken in achieving that performance.
18. The organization views and assesses risk by business unit.
19. The board is engaged in the discussion of strategy and the related risks.
20. The board includes some members who are experts in the organization's relevant risks or risk oversight.
21. The board feels confident in the risk oversight process.
22. The board examines its own talent for diversity of views and the ability to oversee risk.
23. The board examines risks that management missed to determine whether the risk was not identified or not assessed properly. The feedback is used to better manage future risks.
24. The board has good communication with the CEO on the risks facing the enterprise (both current and emerging).
25. The board and management regularly assess their ERM process.

Appendix C

SUMMARY OF CAE/INTERNAL AUDIT'S ROLE IN BOARD RISK OVERSIGHT BEST PRACTICES

1. Internal auditors could make the board presentation or be present when management presents the risks.
2. Internal auditors should be ready to answer board questions related to the risks.
3. Internal auditors could provide assurance on the information provided by management.
4. Internal auditors could provide updates on the status of management's action plans.
5. Consider offering training to board members on the complexities of the business and the associated risk.
6. Consider briefing notes for board members or pre-meetings with board members and/or committee chairs who have risk oversight responsibility.
7. Recommend to those charged with risk oversight which risks or business units should be discussed.
8. Provide analysis or comparisons of risks disclosed by peer organizations.
9. Be aware of board members' backgrounds and skills.
10. Be available to offer risk training.
11. Be ready and available to the board to provide an independent perspective on the business(es) risks and risk management processes.
12. Provide an annual assessment of the ERM process.
13. Provide an assessment of the effectiveness of management's response to the risks.
14. Test the effectiveness of related risk mitigation controls.
15. Provide assurance that the risk oversight structure is appropriate.
16. Provide recommendations or best practices to assist in enhancing the risk management process.
17. Provide a review or assessment of the risk responsibility assignments.
18. Provide an assessment of the strategic risk management process, including performance measurement practices.
19. Provide an independent analysis or assessment of the organization's strategic risks.
20. Know and be ready to provide assessment of the velocity of major risks.

21. Review the risk dashboards and risk heat maps to confirm the velocity assigned to each major risk.
22. Stay current on ERM tools, techniques, and best practices.
23. Benchmark and network with peer groups on risk practices.
24. Provide a briefing of ERM and risk oversight best practices to those charged with risk oversight.
25. Identify conferences or programs on risk practices that would be appropriate for the organization's directors or executives.
26. Provide a periodic assessment or updates of the emerging risks.
27. Stay informed of developments related to the industry and business model that could alter the organization's risk profile.
28. Serve as a catalyst to prompt ongoing discussions with a management working group or committee to discuss emerging risks.
29. Review the organization's current risk reporting for completeness, timeliness, accuracy, and relevance.
30. Compare the organization's reporting to the board best practices listed above.
31. If possible, assist with the deep dive into the risks.
32. Consider whether the "tone at the top" of the organization has negatively impacted risk reporting.
33. Review the organization's proxy risk oversight disclosures as well as its 10-K risk factor disclosures.
34. Compare risk disclosures to peer organizations.
35. Discuss with the external auditors their assessment of the organization's risks.
36. Thoroughly understand your organization's entire ERM process to be able to accurately provide feedback to those charged with risk oversight.
37. Conduct assessments of the adequacy and effectiveness of the organization's risk management processes.
38. Benchmark your organization's ERM process against a widely accepted ERM framework.
39. Assist management in communicating the importance of ERM to the organization.
40. Perform a review of the organization's overall governance process, including risk management processes and reporting, and report accordingly.
41. Ensure that there are appropriate and ongoing communication- and information-sharing processes with the organization's CRO.

Appendix C: Summary of CAE/Internal Audit's Role in Board Risk Oversight Best Practices

42. Assist the organization's risk and control units to identify opportunities to leverage common processes or technologies across the risk and control units.

43. Assess tone or the risk culture across the organization and report accordingly.

44. Be prepared to objectively discuss the organization's tone and risk culture in executive sessions with the audit committee.

Appendix D

INTERVIEW PROTOCOL

A. The board and risk management

1. How aware is the board of the organization's risk management efforts?

2. How does the board measure and communicate the organization's risk appetite and risk tolerance levels? How formal is the process? How does the board ensure that its assessment of risk appetite is in sync with that of the shareholders?

3. Do management and the board understand how the organization's risk profile is changing? Are there concerns that still keep the board "awake at night?" Are appropriate plans in place to manage such risks?

4. To what extent has the board delegated risk management to a subcommittee? What is the subcommittee? Are the delegations clear to all parties? What are the risk oversight roles of the board and respective committees?

5. How would you describe the risk dialog between the board and executive management?

6. How does the organization link strategy to risk oversight and related risks? What are the key drivers of success and the related risks?

B. Tools and approaches used by the board in evaluating the effectiveness of risk management

1. How well does the board monitor the effectiveness of risk management?

2. Does the board receive a comprehensive analysis of risks? How does the organization avoid silo risk management?

3. What specific steps have been taken beyond generating a risk map?

4. To what extent does the board attempt to reach a consensus on risk exposures?

5. Has the board agreed on the top risks? What factors are used to determine a top risk?

6. Which risks does the board quantify and how are the risks quantified?

7. How sophisticated are the organization's risk management processes and tools? How are they structured?

8. How is executive compensation linked to risk? Does that change over time?

9. To what extent are risk metrics and dashboards included in the normal reporting system to the board?

10. Are risks communicated to the board timely?

11. Does the annual budgeting process explicitly use risk information to allocate resources to business units?

12. Does the board currently assess board effectiveness? What tools are currently used? Does the assessment include the risk oversight process?
13. What training have executives and the board received on risk management and risk oversight?
14. Has the board assessed how the risk process enables it to meet its objectives?

C. *Internal audit in the risk management effort*
1. What is the CAE's involvement in risk management? Has this changed over time?
2. What communication/reporting is routinely made to the board by internal audit with respect to risk management?
3. Are you satisfied with internal audit's role in the risk management process?
4. How potentially valuable is internal audit to the risk management process?

Notes

1. National Association of Corporate Directors (NACD), *Key Agreed Principles To Strengthen Corporate Governance for U.S. Publicly Traded Companies*, White Papers: Series I – Risk Oversight, Transparency, Strategy and Executive Compensation (Washington, DC: NACD, 2009), 6.

2. T. L. Barton, W. G. Shenkir, and P. L. Walker, *Making Enterprise Risk Management Pay Off* (Morristown, NJ: Financial Executives Research Foundation, 2001).

3. D. McNamee and G. M. Selim, *Risk Management: Changing the Internal Auditor's Paradigm* (Altamonte Springs, FL: The Institute of Internal Auditors Research Foundation, 1998).

4. L. Nottingham, *A Conceptual Framework for Integrated Risk Management* (Ottawa, ON: The Conference Board of Canada, 1997).

5. Barton, Shenkir, and Walker, *Making Enterprise Risk Management Pay Off*.

6. P. L. Walker, W. G. Shenkir, and T. L. Barton, *Enterprise Risk Management: Pulling It All Together* (Altamonte Springs, FL: The Institute of Internal Auditors Research Foundation, 2002).

7. R. Scott, W. G. Shenkir, and P. L. Walker, *Enterprise-Wide Risk Management: Recommendations to COSO* (2000).

8. The Institute of Internal Auditors (IIA), *Standards for the Professional Practice of Internal Auditing* (Altamonte Springs, FL: The Institute of Internal Auditors, 2001).

9. IIA, *Standards*, 2.

10. G.P. Coetzee and R. du Bruyn, "The Relationship between the New IIA Standards and the Internal Auditing Profession," *Meditari Accountancy Research* (Vol. 9, 2001), 66.

11. IIA, *Standards*, 10.

12. For example, see the letter to the SEC by Walker (http://www.sec.gov/rules/proposed/s74002/plwalker1.htm) and the letter by Jeff Thompson, President of the IMA, to the SEC at http://www.sec.gov/comments/s7-24-06/s72406-12.pdf.

13. U.S. Securities and Exchange Commission, *Final Rule: Management's Reports on Internal Control Over Financial Reporting and Certification of Disclosure in Exchange Act Periodic Reports*, effective August 2003, 9.

14. Martin Lipton, "Risk Management and the Board of Directors," *The Harvard Law School Forum on Corporate Governance and Financial Regulation* (blog), December 17, 2009.

15. Ibid.

16. W. G. Shenkir and P. L. Walker, *Enterprise Risk Management* (Washington, DC: BNA, 2007) 138.

17. Shenkir and Walker, *Enterprise Risk Management*, 141.

18. Shenkir and Walker, *Enterprise Risk Management*, 148.

19 Shenkir and Walker, *Enterprise Risk Management,* 155.

20 Institute of Directors in Southern Africa (IoDSA), *King Report on Corporate Governance for South Africa* (Johannesburg: IoDSA, 2002), 6.

21 Committee of Sponsoring Organizations of the Treadway Commission (COSO), *Enterprise Risk Management – Integrated Framework: Executive Summary* (New York: AICPA, 2004), 3.

22 P. L. Walker, W. G. Shenkir, and T. L. Barton, *Proxy Disclosure Enhancements and ERM Opportunities,* Financial Executives International Issue Alert (Morristown, NJ: Financial Executives Institute, April 2010), 3.

23 NACD, *Key Agreed Principles to Strengthen Corporate Governance,* 3.

24 Mark L. Frigo and Richard J. Anderson, "Embracing Enterprise Risk Management: Practical Approaches for Getting Started" (COSO, 2011), 6.

25 Ibid.

26 Committee of Sponsoring Organizations of the Treadway Commission (COSO), *Enterprise Risk Management – Integrated Framework: Executive Summary,* 2.

27 International Organization for Standardization, *ISO 31000, Risk Management – Principles and Guidelines* (Geneva, Switzerland: ISO, 2009), 4.3.4.

28 T. Nagumo, "Aligning Enterprise Risk Management with Strategy through the BSC: The Bank of Tokyo-Mitsubishi Approach," *Balanced Scorecard Report* (September-October 2005: Reprint No. B0509D), 4.

29 Ibid.

30 P. Kocourek, R.V. Lee, C. Kelly, and J. Newfrock, "Too Much SOX Can Kill You," *Strategy+Business* (January 2004).

31 Economist Intelligence Unit, *Enterprise Risk Management – Implementing New Solutions* (New York, 2001), 8.

32 S. M. Davis and J. Lukomnik, "Risk Velocity, The Unknown Dimension in ERM," *Compliance Week,* December 8, 2009.

33 Ibid.

34 The Corporate Executive Board, "Enterprise Risk Intelligence: The Latest Challenges and Recommended Solutions for ERM Executives," Marketing Materials, April 2010, Appendix, 2–3.

35 Microsoft Corporation, Form 10-K for the fiscal year ended June 30, 2007, 21.

36 Microsoft, 2007 10-K, 15.

37 S. Hansell, "Steve Ballmer Maps Microsoft's Cloud-y Future," *New York Times* (March 20, 2009).

38 "Top 5 Cloud Security Questions for CIOs," *CIO* (April 8, 2011).

39 ISO 31000, 4.3.6.

40 ISO 31000, A.3.4.

Notes

41 Walker, Shenkir and Barton, *Proxy Disclosure Enhancements*.

42 Pioneering ERM efforts are documented in Barton, Shenkir and Walker, *Making Enterprise Risk Management Pay Off* and Walker, Shenkir and Barton, *Enterprise Risk Management: Pulling it All Together*, respectively.

43 Standard & Poor's (S&P), *Progress Report: Integrating Enterprise Risk Management Analysis Into Corporate Credit Ratings* (New York: S&P, 2009), 2.

44 Senior Supervisors Group (SSG), *Observations on Risk Management Practices during the Recent Market Turbulence* (New York: SSG, 2008), 9.

45 ISO 31000, 2.

46 COSO Executive Summary, 4–5.

47 ISO 31000, v.

48 Parkour is a discipline in which an individual traverses his surroundings quickly using physical resources as are immediately available. It places a premium on quick reflexes and agility.

49 Barton, Shenkir, and Walker, *Making Enterprise Risk Management Pay Off*.

50 Walker, Shenkir, and Barton, *Proxy Disclosure Enhancements*.

51 See the full guidelines at http://ftp.ussc.gov/2010guid/8b2 1.htm. These guidelines set the requirements for an effective compliance and ethics program. The guidelines were written in response to section 805 (a)(2)(5) of the U.S. Sarbanes-Oxley Act of 2002.

52 The Institute of Internal Auditors (IIA), *The Role of Internal Auditing in Enterprise-wide Risk Management*, Position Statement (Altamonte Springs, FL: The Institute of Internal Auditors, 2004), 3.

53 Ibid.

54 The Institute of Internal Auditors (IIA), *Assessing the Adequacy of Risk Management Processes*, Practice Advisory 2120-1 (Altamonte Springs, FL: The Institute of Internal Auditors, 2009).

The vision of The IIA Research Foundation is to understand, shape, and advance the global profession of internal auditing by initiating and sponsoring intelligence gathering, innovative research, and knowledge-sharing in a timely manner. As a separate, tax-exempt organization, The Foundation does not receive funding from IIA membership dues but depends on contributions from individuals and organizations, and from IIA chapters and institutes, to move our programs forward. We also would not be able to function without our valuable volunteers. To that end, we thank the following:

Research Sponsor Recognition

Research Sponsors

Chicago Chapter

Houston Chapter

IIA Netherlands

Philadelphia Chapter

Principal Partners

Strategic Partners:

ACL Services Ltd.

CCH® TeamMate

Partners:

CaseWare IDEA Inc.

Ernst & Young LLP

PricewaterhouseCoopers LLP

Visionary Circle

The Family of Lawrence B. Sawyer

Chairman's Circle

Michael J. Head, CIA   ExxonMobil Corporation

Stephen D. Goepfert, CIA   Itau Unibanco Holding S.A.

Patricia E. Scipio, CIA   JCPenney Company, Inc.

Paul J. Sobel, CIA   Lockheed Martin Corporation

                                Southern California Edison Company

Diamond Donor

Central Ohio Chapter

New York Chapter

San Jose Chapter

THE IIA RESEARCH FOUNDATION BOARD OF TRUSTEES

President: Patricia E. Scipio, CIA, *PricewaterhouseCoopers LLP*
Vice President-Strategy: Richard J. Anderson, CFSA, *DePaul University*
Vice President-Research and Education: Philip E. Flora, CIA, CCSA, *FloBiz & Associates, LLC*
Vice President-Development: Wayne G. Moore, CIA, *Wayne Moore Consulting*
Treasurer: Mark J. Pearson, CIA, *Boise Inc.*
Secretary: Michael F. Pryal, CIA, *Federal Signal Corporation*

Neil Aaron, *The McGraw-Hill Companies*
Urton L. Anderson, PhD, CIA, CCSA, CFSA, CGAP, *University of Texas-Austin*
Audley Bell, *Habitat for Humanity International*
Sten Bjelke, CIA, *IIA Sweden*
Peter H. G. Cheng, *National Health Research Institutes*
Jacques Lapointe, *Province of Nova Scotia*
James A. LaTorre, *PricewaterhouseCoopers LLP*
Kasurthrie Justine Mazzocco, *IIA – South Africa*
Betty L. McPhilimy, *Northwestern University*
Wayne G. Moore, *Wayne Moore Consulting*
John Pierson, *Deloitte & Touche LLC*
Jeffrey Perkins, CIA, *TransUnion LLC*
Edward C. Pitts, *Avago Technologies*
Larry E. Rittenberg, PhD, CIA, *University of Wisconsin*
Mark L. Salamasick, CIA, *University of Texas at Dallas*
Susan D. Ulrey, CIA, *KPMG LLP*
Jacqueline K. Wagner, CIA, *Ernst & Young LLP*
Shi Xian, *Nanjing Audit University*
Douglas Ziegenfuss, PhD, CIA, CCSA, *Old Dominion University*

THE IIA RESEARCH FOUNDATION COMMITTEE OF RESEARCH AND EDUCATION ADVISORS

Chairman:

Philip E. Flora, CIA, CCSA, *FloBiz & Associates, LLC*

Vice-chairman:

Urton L. Anderson, PhD, CIA, CCSA, CFSA, CGAP, *University of Texas-Austin*

Members

Barry B. Ackers, *University of South Africa*

James A. Alexander, CIA, *Unitus Community Credit Union*

Lalbahadur Balkaran, CIA, *Independent Internal Audit Consultant*

John Beeler, *SalesForce.com Inc*

Joseph P. Bell, CIA, CGAP, *Ohio Office of Internal Audit*

Sharon Bell, CIA, *Internal Audit Services Manager*

Toby Bishop, *Deloitte & Touche LLP (US)*

Sezer Bozkus, *KPMG EUROPE*

John K. Brackett, CFSA, *RSM McGladrey, Inc*

Adil S. Buhariwala, CIA, *IIA — United Arab Emirates*

Jean Coroller

Mary Christine Dobrovich, *Experis Finance*

Susan Page Driver, CIA, *Texas General Land Office*

Donald A. Espersen, CIA, *despersen & associate*

Peter Funck, *IIA — Sweden*

John C. Gazlay

Ulrich Hahn, CIA, CCSA, CGAP

John C. Harris, CIA, *Markel Aspen/FirstComp Insurance Company*

Sabrina B. Hearn, CIA, *University of Alabama System*

Karin L. Hill, CIA, CGAP, *Texas Youth Commission*

Katherine E. Sidway Homer, CIA, *Ernst & Young LLP*

David J. MacCabe, CIA, CGAP, *Consultant*

Michael Malcolm, CIA, CFSA, *Research in Motion (RIM)*

Steve Mar, CFSA, *Nordstrom*

John D. McLaughlin, *BDO*

Deborah L. Munoz, CIA, *CalPortland Cement Company*

Frank O'Brien, CIA, *Olin Corporation*

Michael L. Piazza, *Professional Development Associates*

Amy Jane Prokopetz, CCSA, *Farm Credit Canada*

Vito Raimondi, CIA, *Zurich Financial Services NA*

Sandra W. Shelton, *DePaul University*

Tania Stegemann, CIA, CCSA, *Rio Tinto*

Warren W. Stippich Jr., CIA, *Grant Thornton Chicago*

Stig J. Sunde, CIA, CGAP, *IIA — United Arab Emirates*

David Williams, *JCPenney Company Inc*

Valerie Wolbrueck, CIA, *Lennox International Inc*

Linda Yanta, CIA, *Eskom*